GROW
COOK
EAT

A GIY guide to
growing and
cooking your
own food

GROW COOK EAT

A GIY guide to growing and cooking your own food

MICHAEL KELLY

edited by
Cristíona Kiely

First Published by GIY Ireland (Activities) Ltd in 2014.
Second edition published by GIY Ireland (Activities) Ltd in 2017.
ISBN 978-0-9930426-1-4

First Published by GIY Ireland (Activities) Ltd in 2014.

Second edition published by GIY Ireland (Activities) Ltd in 2017.

A CIP catalogue record for this book is available from the British Library.

ISBN 978-0-9930426-1-4

Printed on FSC certified paper

Editor **Cristíona Kiely**

Copy-editor **Mícheál Ó Cadhla**

Designer **Lucy Parissi**

Design Editor **Jessica Reid**

Index compiled by **Eileen O'Neill**

Printed by **Printer Trento, SRL, Italy**

Important note to readers.

The information contained in this book is intended as a general guide. Many plants, herbs, seaweeds and fungi, whether used externally or internally, can cause an allergic reaction in some people. Before trying any remedies, herbal or otherwise, the reader is recommended to sample a small quantity first to establish if there is an adverse reaction. Please seek out medical advice in the case of an adverse reaction. Neither the author, editor or publisher can be held responsible for any adverse reactions to the recipes, instructions or advice given in the book. Use of any ingredients is entirely at the reader's own risk.

Michael Kelly is founder of GIY. He has written columns on food and health for The Irish Times, The Irish Independent and Food & Wine Magazine. This is his third book, following Trading Paces (2008) and Tales from the Home Farm (2009). Michael is presenter with Karen O'Donohoe of the RTE 1 TV series GROW COOK EAT, which was filmed on location at GROW HQ in Waterford.

Michael is a member of the Irish Food Writers Guild and The Taste Council, and received the 'Local Food Hero' award at the 2017 Irish Restaurant Awards. He worked in the IT industry in Dublin for ten years, but a chance meeting with a bulb of Chinese garlic put him on the road to the good life. He now lives in Dunmore East with his wife Eilish and two little GIYers. He grows his own food, often badly.

The first edition of GROW COOK EAT received a Gourmand World Cookbook Award.

CONTENTS

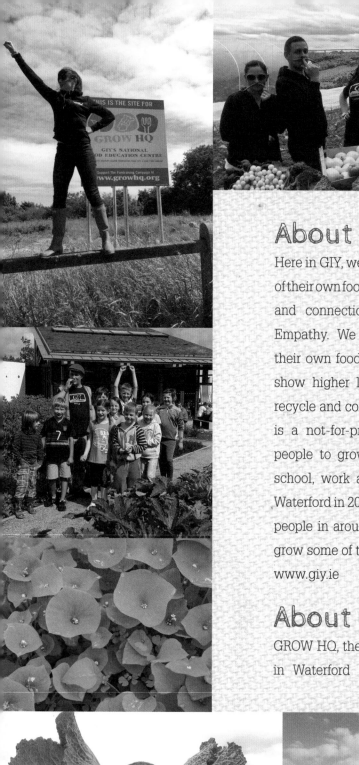

About GIY

Here in GIY, we believe that when people grow some of their own food they develop a deeper understanding and connection with food which we call Food Empathy. We know that people who grow some of their own food have better diets and eating habits; show higher levels of knowledge about nutrition; recycle and compost more, and waste less food. GIY is a not-for-profit social enterprise that supports people to grow some of their own food at home, school, work and in the community. Founded in Waterford in 2008, each year we now support 500,000 people in around 9,000 community food projects to grow some of their own food for the first time. www.giy.ie

About GROW HQ

GROW HQ, the home of the GIY movement, opened in Waterford in October 2016 and has quickly

established itself as a centre of excellence for home-grown and local food as well as a beacon of positivity and good health in our community. GROW HQ has an award-winning café/bistro, shop and education centre in a stunning eco-building, and 3 acres of food production and teaching gardens. GROW HQ won the national Farm to Plate Award at the 2017 Food & Wine Awards. www.growhq.org.

GROW COOK EAT TV

From Spring 2018, GROW HQ is the set for a brand new 7-part GIY TV series (called GROW COOK EAT), to be aired on RTE 1 television. Presented by Michael Kelly and Karen O'Donohoe the series brings viewers on a plot-to-plate journey through the growing year. Series 1 is sponsored by Bord Bia and the EPA.

FOREWORD

I'VE JUST HARVESTED MY FIRST CROP OF RASPBERRIES. For me, summer officially starts when these crimson-coloured fruits are ripe to eat. Low in sugar, packed full of vitamin C and other health-giving compounds, these succulent nuggets are in high demand and the long wait has been worth it. "Once you've tasted the magic, there's no going back", says Michael Kelly about growing food. Never a truer word.

I've long thought that Michael Kelly's disenchantment with life was a godsend. His abandonment of city living in favour of a windswept acre in rural Waterford heralded the start of the development of something quite profound: a lively community-based food movement that galvanises people to grow food for themselves, and each other.

Michael and the GIY movement reawakened in us what has always been there, even in a dormant state. For the vast majority of human existence, we lived on food that came from within a couple of miles of where we lived. Until the start of the twentieth century, people mainly grew their own food or bought foods that were locally produced. By the end of the century, patterns of consumption had utterly changed, with the expansion of supermarkets, fast-food outlets and convenience centres.

The price we've paid is a food system so complex it is almost inconceivable. Who feeds us? What would a map of the global food system look like? These are not unreasonable questions to ask. But in 2009, when the UK government drew on the knowledge of hundreds of experts in search of answers, they were defeated. "We gave up", admitted the project leader. "It was too complicated".

We have to eat to live, but how we want to live is the most important question facing us all. The things that the modern food system has freed us from - such as growing and cooking - are, on reflection, the very things we should value and keep. We are grappling with an overweight and obesity epidemic, high levels of diabetes and heart disease and an escalating and devastating problem of food poverty. Add the frightening spectre of climate change to that mix and it's clear that the role of food in health is a blaring wake-up call for us all. The astonishing success of GIY is an indication that change is happening. Deciding to put a seed in the soil and to grow - and cook - your own food is a vote for a healthy, nourishing life.

This book is a growing and cookery bible rolled into one, written by the best in the business. But fundamentally it's about something more profound than that: our collective health. The GIY movement urges us to grow it, cook it, eat it. We do lots of the (delicious!) final bit; for the good of our health, and that of our environment, it's time to get stuck into the rest.

Ella McSweeney

INTRODUCTION

It would be nice if I could say that this book is the last you will ever need to buy on the subject of food growing, but it's unlikely to be that. I would love to be able to point to my many decades of horticultural experience and my vast knowledge of the Latin names for plants. But alas, I can't do that either.

I will start with a confession. Before I started growing my own food nine years ago, my green-fingered claim-to-fame was that I was highly skilled at killing bonsai trees. I went through a phase in my twenties where I considered them to be the coolest thing on this planet. Sadly, by the time my love affair ended, I had killed five trees with a collective age of over 3,000 years.

So, let me tell you my garlic story, for that is where it all began. I was working in the IT industry at the time, and in the local supermarket doing the weekly shop, absentmindedly about to throw a net of garlic in the trolley when I noticed that it said "Product of China" on the label.

That was my Road to Damascus moment – I had never seen a food import from China before and the fact that it was something so small and so cheap that had travelled SO far, just really got my goat up. The Chinese garlic is a metaphor for all that is wrong with our food chain, which is no longer really about food, seasonality or feeding ourselves. It's about a global trade system that in many ways has devastating consequences for our health, local employment and this little planet that we all share.

Being a contrary git and in a valiant attempt to stick it to the man, I decided to grow my own garlic. If you have grown your own garlic before, you will know that it's a very simple thing to do really. You stick a clove in the soil, and over time that clove splits and becomes a bulb - voila! So, in a way I was lucky I started with garlic and not something more challenging to grow like carrots.

Having stuck some cloves of garlic in the ground, I waited. As it grows, garlic sends up a nice green shoot, which eventually grows to a couple of feet in height. In my innocence I assumed the garlic bulb would grow ON TOP of the shoot and when that failed to materialize, I grew increasingly despondent. Then one day the shoot started to go yellow. Then it fell over. This in fact is garlic's way of telling you that the bulb is now ready to be plucked from the ground.

But I just thought it was dead.

I got my shiniest spade from the garage to dig up my sad garlic experiment – low and behold, underneath the soil there was a magnificent bulb of garlic. In my mind it was the size of an orange, but the garlic story has grown some legs over the years, so I can't be sure it was really that big.

Heady with success, and considering myself quite the champion grower, I resolved to try and produce as much of my own food as I could. And so in our garden we embraced the good life, growing all manner of veg, herbs and fruit; rearing some animals (pigs, chickens and turkeys) for the table; keeping hens and ducks for eggs and bees for honey. Nine years later, I am still waiting for my experience to catch up with my enthusiasm but it's been quite the adventure.

The idea of the first GIY group (set up in Waterford in 2008) was to encourage other people to grow their own food and to surround myself with people that knew more about food growing than I did. I had gone looking for a grower's group to join so I could share the journey with like-minded people but found only plant clubs. Since I had little interest in general gardening, and because I'm a sucker for a harebrained project, I decided to set up a food grower's group myself.

Little did I realize that our little local project would eventually become a sizeable not-for-profit movement of amateur food growers in Ireland, the UK and further afield - at the time of writing, over 500,000 people coming together each year to grow food at home, school, work and in the community. That GIY now has its very own home, the fabulous GROW HQ in Waterford city, and creates employment for nearly 30 people, is a source of immense pride for me..

Over the years I've written hundreds of thousands of words on GIYing for our website and for newspapers and magazines. Sometimes I feel that I do more writing and talking about growing than actual growing. I figured it was about time to pull the best bits together in to some form of useful guide on the subject. This book is not trying to be GIY's comprehensive A-Z guide – what it is, is an honest account of my food growing efforts, based on growing well over 40 different types of veg each year – which works well enough for me and produces a shed-load of food. Since it's based on how I do things in my own veg patch, you might find the approach a little different to other books about food growing.

Every year I have my share of triumphs and tragedies in the veg patch. That's OK. Like most GIYers, I am not interested in complete self-sufficiency. I grow as much food as I can, but I am constrained by lack of time and expertise. I still go to the supermarket on a weekly basis, and I don't beat myself up over that. I don't have to buy as much food as I used too, and that makes me happy. At some times of the year I don't have to buy any vegetables or fruit at all, and that makes me happier still.

Becoming a GIYer has allowed me to take a look under the bonnet so to speak and understand how it all works. That knowledge has had a profound knock-on impact in other areas of my life. I am healthier, and live more sustainably. As a family, our diet has improved – we eat more plants and less meat. Growing my own has made me a better-informed consumer, so that when I do buy food, I buy more seasonal, local and organic produce.

In GIY we call this deeper understanding, food empathy. Interestingly, food empathy seems to arise for people regardless of how much food they grow which means the person growing some food on a balcony is just as important to the movement as the 10-acre smallholder.

You might well ask – why in a book about growing food are there so many recipes? My answer is – why not? When we grow food, surely the end point that we have in mind is that we will cook it and then eat it? Too often in my view, when people talk or write about food growing, it's done in the 'gardening' context, lumped in with information about keeping your dahlias fresh (or whatever it is you do with dahlias). Food growing is always in the 'gardening' column in the weekend newspaper and food-growing books are always in the gardening section of the book shop.

Undoubtedly, for many people food growing is indeed a pleasurable gardening activity. But for many others, including me, it's not really about gardening at all – it's about food. It's about nutrition, wellbeing, and living sustainably. The horticultural haughtiness (which let's be honest, can be an occasional hallmark)

is in fact a real turn off. So this is, unashamedly, a book about food – pure and simple. Growing it, cooking it, eating it. Understanding it. Loving it.

It's been amazing to see this book reach a broad audience since it was first published in 2014 and I was immensely proud to see it win a Gourmand World Cookbook Award. The fact that it will now become a companion piece for a new RTE TV series of the same name proves I think that the original concept had merit. I am delighted to welcome JB Dubois, our Head Chef at GROW HQ and Jess Murphy (who features in the show) to the contributing chef list.

I am more excited than ever at the potential for food growing to change lives and maybe even the world – that surely sounds hopelessly naive, but it's how I feel. I have learned my optimism from the process of veg growing itself - you place a seed in the soil in the cold winter and it seems unlikely that such a little speck of a thing could ever become food. Eventually however it confounds you and becomes exactly that. Come on the journey with us. The future belongs to those of us willing to get our hands dirty.

CONTRIBUTORS

As a GIYer, one of the key challenges (and delights) for me is to have great recipes to turn my hard-earned homegrown food in to great meals. There are undoubtedly some amazing books out there about growing, and there are also phenomenal cookbooks. More rare, is a book that blurs the lines between the growing and cooking, which is really odd when you think about it.

When Cristíona (my editor) and I sat down to plan out this book, we wanted to include recipes which GIYers would really appreciate and find useful. Our initial idea was to include one recipe for each month. Since I'm no great chef myself, I said; "Hey, why don't we see if we can get some of our patrons and other famous chefs to contribute the recipes? Better that than we end up poisoning people with my recipe ideas!" How we laughed.

Thinking that perhaps not everyone would agree to have their recipes included, we asked WAY more people than we needed. I clearly recall how excited we were the week the responses started coming in from these amazing chefs, cooks and growers saying they would love to come on board. Cristíona and I were sending each other texts and emails saying things like: "Hugh's on board", "Clodagh's on board", "Dylan's on board" etc. A little over a week later, feeling stunned and incredibly grateful, and with over 35 contributors confirmed, we realized a few things: (a) we would need a much, much bigger book than we had planned, (b) this would almost certainly be the first time that these amazing people would come together under one book cover, and as a result (c) we suddenly had a monumental, crushing responsibility for the book to live up to the quality of the contributors.

We also knew that our biggest challenge would be to create a sense of flow and continuity with such a diverse group of contributors, each one bringing their own writing style and approach to recipes. We have presented all the recipes here as they were originally printed, and hope you will celebrate that diversity as being part of the spirit of the book!

I am still pinching myself that such an incredible group of people wanted to get involved – a testament I think to the great reputation that GIY has built over many years, thanks to our hardworking staff and volunteers. As a bit of a hacker grower myself, I am particularly humbled to have such renowned growers like Joy Larkcom, Alys Fowler, Hugh Fearnley Whittingstall and Mark Diacono in a book with my name on it.

It's fitting that Darina Allen is the first contributor you will see profiled overleaf. I recall Darina showing up at one of the first GIY Waterford meetings in 2009. We had no reputation to speak of at the time, but Darina showed up because she liked the GIY group idea, and wanted to give her time (and name) to support us. She has been a patron of GIY ever since, and has given more to the cause than I could have dared ask.

We are absolutely indebted to each and every contributor for turning this book in to something very, very special indeed. They were generous to a fault with their time, their creativity, and above all their passion for great food. We are also very grateful to the many publishers for giving us permission to re-print them and the photographers who allowed us to profile their great work. Thank you one and all.

– Michael Kelly

DARINA ALLEN, owner of *Ballymaloe Cookery School* in Shanagarry, Co Cork, Ireland, is a teacher, food writer, newspaper columnist, cookbook author and television presenter. She is a member of the International SLOW FOOD Movement, is a best-selling author, and has presented eight series of her cookery programmes *Simply Delicious* on television in Ireland. A tireless ambassador for Irish food both at home and abroad, Darina has also been instrumental in setting up the Farmers Market movement in Ireland.

RACHEL ALLEN is a busy TV chef, author, columnist and mother, and still teaches at *Ballymaloe Cookery School*. Rachel is the author of twelve bestselling cookery books, and her television series for RTE and the BBC have been broadcast internationally in 33 different countries. She lives near Ballymaloe in County Cork with her husband Isaac, sons Lucca and Joshua and daughter Scarlett Lily.

CATHAL ARMSTRONG Chef and co-owner of *Restaurant Eve* (in Alexandria, Virginia, US), Cathal Armstrong was born into a Dublin family with a passion for food. As a result of his travels and experiences he is dedicated to the ideals of environmentalism, health and conservation. In 2011 he was honoured as a *Champion of Change*, under President Obama's Winning the Future initiative. Cathal's first book came out in 2014. *My Irish Table*, features recipes showcasing modern Irish fare, interlaced with stories about his journey from Dublin to Washington, DC.

DORCAS BARRY teaches cookery classes with a focus on healthy food and has a diploma in Clinical Nutrition as well as being a qualified detox coach. She has completed a raw food chef course and continues to study raw, vegan and vegetarian food and how they can contribute to a healthy diet. Dorcas works with companies to run Healthy Eating events in the workplace, including collaborating with chefs to develop recipes for staff.

DERRY CLARKE, has been Chef/Patron of *l'Ecrivain* for over 25 years, having opened it in 1989 with his wife Sallyanne. Derry, and *l'Ecrivain* have been awarded many accolades over the past 21 years, such as Best Restaurant and Best Chef Awards since 1999. *l'Ecrivain* also has a Michelin Star which was first awarded in 2003. Derry promotes the use of organic and non-GMO foods. His food ethos is simple: he uses the finest of fresh local produce.

DENIS COTTER, best known for his creative vegetarian cuisine in Cork's renowned *Cafe Paradiso*, is an experienced cookery teacher and food consultant as well as the author of four award-winning cookbooks. His first book *The Café Paradiso Cookbook* was shortlisted for the British Guild of Food Writers Awards. *Paradiso Seasons* won Best Vegetarian Cookbook in the World at the Gourmand World Cookbook Awards in Barcelona in 2004. His third book *wild garlic, gooseberries & me* was shortlisted for the Andre Simon Awards in 2008. His most recent book *for the love of food* was published by Harper Collins in 2011.

MICHELLE DARMODY is proprietor of *The Cake Cafe*, food writer with the Irish Examiner, author of *The Cake Cafe Bake Book* and is a regular judge on Masterchef. Michelle studied fine art but grew up with a love of good quality food which was handed down to her from her parents. Michelle has recently been on the judging panel for The Arthur Guinness Projects. She has opened a second premises in Stoneybatter, Dublin 7 and has launched a range of Irish-made home-wares that won two ICAD awards for their design.Through her publishing house Michelle has recently launched a food quarterly called *Slice*.

TRISH DESEINE– Born and raised in Northern Ireland, after graduating from Edinburgh University Trish moved to Paris in the 80s and has lived in and around the city ever since. She is a cookbook author and restaurant reviewer and was named one of French Vogue's 40 women of the decade in 2010. Her TV cooking series' include *Trish's Paris Kitchen* and her biggest publishing success, *Je Veux du Chocolat*, a book of very simple chocolate recipes was translated into 9 languages.

MARK DIACONO is an award-winning writer and photographer. Known for his commitment to sustainable, ethically produced food, Mark was head of the Garden Team at Hugh Fearnley-Whittingstall's River Cottage for many years before setting up Otter Farm, Britain's first and only climate change farm. Mark has written six award winning books, including this year's *A Year at Otter Farm* and 2011's *A Taste of the Unexpected* (Food Book of the Year 2011).

TOM & JOHANN DOORLEY have been married for 30 years and live on a hillside on the Cork/Waterford border where they grow their own vegetables and fruit. They wrote Grow & Cook in 2007 about what they do with their produce in the kitchen. Tom is food and wine columnist with the Irish Daily Mail, a contributor to *www.TheDiningRoom.ie* and Johann teaches cookery in Cork and blogs as Zanzarella Caccabus.

JB DUBOIS is Head Chef at GROW HQ, the home of the GIY movement. From the small town of Luneville, in the north east of France, JB moved to Ireland to work in Galway 17 years ago, and fell in love immediately with the quality and diversity of Irish produce. He has a wealth of experience in boutique and 5-star hotels and restaurants, and a strong focus on fresh, local, seasonal products of impeccable quality. He combines this with a lifelong love of traditional methods of preserving veg like pickling and fermenting. Using produce grown right outside the door in his home-made meals, sauces, ketchups, vinegars, krauts and preserves is a dream come true for this chef.

KEVIN DUNDON is the Chef/Proprietor of *Dunbrody Country House Hotel & Restaurant*, located in Ireland's sunny South East. *Dunbrody* was established in 1997 by Kevin and his wife Catherine. Kevin has published four books, *Full on Irish, Great Family Food, Recipes that Work* and *Modern Irish Food* to accompany his TV series Kevin *Dundon's Modern Irish Food* on RTÉ. He has also launched his own App *For the Love of Food*. Kevin and Catherine have three Children; Emily, Sophie and Tom.

HUGH FEARNLEY-WHITTINGSTALL is widely known as a writer, broadcaster and campaigner with an uncompromising commitment to real and sustainable food. His many series for Channel 4, and his best-selling *River Cottage* books, have earned him a huge popular following. Hugh and his team of food experts operate out of *River Cottage HQ*. HQ is now a venue for courses and events expounding the *River Cottage* food philosophy and celebrating the very best local, seasonal food. Hugh's website, www.rivercottage.net, is an important forum for discussing food issues of every kind.

PAUL FLYNN is the owner of *The Tannery Restaurant*, Dungarvan, Co. Waterford and, as a chef, is renowned for cooking modern Irish food. In 2005 Paul opened *The Tannery Townhouse*, followed soon after by *The Tannery Cookery School and Garden*. He has won numerous awards and features regularly on RTE. His second book, *Second Helpings*, covers a selection of spectacular recipes using seasonal food.

ALYS FOWLER started gardening in her early teens and trained at the Royal Horticultural Society, the New York Botanical Gardens and the Royal Botanic Gardens at Kew. She was a presenter for BBC's *Gardeners' World* and had her own BBC TV series *The Edible Garden*. She writes for *The Guardian*, BBC's *Gardeners' World* magazine and *Gardens Illustrated* as well as publishing her own books, *The Thrifty Gardener*, *Garden Anywhere*, *The Edible Garden*, *The Thrifty Forager* and *Abundance*. She continues her passion to fuse traditional gardening with modern eco-friendly culture.

CATHERINE FULVIO is an award-winning food writer, TV Chef & proprietor of *Ballyknocken House & Cookery School*, in Co. Wicklow. Born and raised on a working farm, Catherine has an inherent knowledge and understanding of food and cherishes the land and its produce. Passionate about ingredients, Catherine prides herself on her extensive herb gardens, vegetable plot and soft fruit garden. Her cookery classes in *Ballyknocken Cookery School* include a tour of the vegetable and herb gardens where ingredients are gathered along the way.

SHARON HEARNE-SMITH has worked as a food stylist and writer for over 17 years in the UK, US and Ireland. Her experience includes work on cookbooks, magazines, advertising, movies and over 30 cookery series with some of the top celebrity chefs. Sharon has recently turned to writing and styling her own cookbook. *No Bake Baking*, which was photographed by Donal Skehan, was published worldwide in June 2014 by her London publishers Quercus.

LILLY HIGGINS is a food writer, photographer and author of *Dream Deli* and *Make Bake Love*, both published by Gill & MacMillan. Lilly writes regularly for newspapers and magazines including *The Sunday Business Post* and *Image Interiors & Living* magazine. Having graduated from *Ballymaloe Cookery School* Lilly went on to teach at the school. Finally using her degree in design as well as her love of baking and cooking Lilly started a food blog in 2010 which has lead to a career in food writing, styling and photography as well as a year spent running an underground supper club in Dublin. Lilly lives in Cobh, Co.Cork with her partner Colm and two small sons.

GEMMA HUGHES is a naturopathic herbalist, who qualified in 2014. She is a keen gardener in Waterford and is a volunteer for Waterford GIY. She has a love for edible, health-improving gardening and teaches people how to utilise their garden vegetables, herbs, shrubs and trees to maintain a healthy and happy body.

MARTIJN KAJUITER– Martijn Kajuiter is a Dutch Michelin Star winning head chef with *The House* in *The Cliff House Hotel* in Ardmore, County Waterford. In 1991, aged 17, he started his kitchen career in *Les Quatre Canetons*, and progressed to positions with John Burton Race, Michel Roux, Piere Koffmann and Marco Pierre White. In 1998 he returned to *Les Quatre Canetons*. In 2000, he became head chef of restaurant *Kwekerij de Kas* in Amsterdam. Martin came to Ireland in 2007 to become Executive Chef of the *Cliff House Hotel* where he earned a Michelin star in 2010. He is married with two children.

DOMINI KEMP trained as a chef at *Leith's* in London, and co-founded *itsa* in 1999, which has grown into 17 different food businesses across Ireland, including *Hatch & Sons* and *Joe's* coffee shop. She is food-writer for *The Irish Times* and publishes her fourth cook-book, *Dinner* in 2014. The Kemp sisters won the IMAGE *Businesswoman of the Year* award, November 2009, and were finalists for the Ernst & Young Entrepreneur of the Year award, in 2011. They are developing a health, juice and whole foods concept for 2014, called *Alchemy Juice Co.*

MARIAN KEYES is the UK's most popular writer of women's fiction. Her international bestselling novels include *Rachel's Holiday, Last Chance Saloon, Sushi for Beginners, Angels, The Other Side of the Story, Anybody Out There, This Charming Man* and *The Brightest Star in the Sky.* Two collections of her journalism, *Under the Duvet* and *Further Under the Duvet,* are also available from Penguin. Marian lives in Dublin with her husband. *Saved by Cake* is an extremely honest account of Marian Keyes' recent battle with depression, and how baking has helped her.

JOY LARKCOM Joy Larkcom's seminal work *Grow your own Vegetables* is the bible for vegetable growers everywhere. One of the world's most respected growers and gardening writers, Joy has been researching, growing and writing about vegetables for over 40 years. Retired to a windy site in West Cork in 2002, Joy has been awarded the RHS Veitch Memorial Medal and the Garden Writer's Guild Lifetime Award.

ROSS LEWIS is from Cork, a graduate of University College Cork, a Michelin star winning head chef and co-owner of the restaurant *Chapter One.* He has travelled and worked in the restaurant industry in New York, London and Switzerland. His passion and drive to open his own restaurant brought him back to Ireland where he became immersed in Ireland's emerging food culture. Ross is a commissioner of Eurotoques and sits on the Taste Council of Ireland.

NEVEN MAGUIRE is proprietor/Head Chef of *MacNean House & Restaurant* and the *Neven Maguire Cookery School* in Blacklion, Co. Cavan. Neven took over *MacNean House & Restaurant* in 2001 and it is now one of Ireland's top restaurants, consistently winning awards for both its cuisine and service. Fulfilling a long-held dream, Neven opened his *Neven Maguire Cookery School* alongside his restaurant in January 2014. Neven Maguire is regarded as one of Ireland's most talented and innovative chefs. www.nevenmaguire.com.

IMEN MCDONNELL is a food and lifestyle columnist for the *Irish Farmers Journal* and *Irish Country Magazine*. In a former life, she spent her days working in broadcast production while living in New York, Minneapolis and Los Angeles. She now resides with her husband and son on their family farm in rural Ireland and shares stories of farm life and food on her popular blog, Farmette.ie. Imen's modern Irish recipes have been featured in *The New York Times*, *The Irish Times*, *The Sunday Times (UK)* *The Los Angeles Times*, *Saveur Magazine* and more. Her first book, *Farmette, Stories and Recipes from Life on an Irish Farm* will be published by ROOST BOOKS in Autumn 2015.

DYLAN MCGRATH is Chef / Proprietor of *Fade Street Social* and *Rustic Stone* restaurants in Dublin City Centre. Dylan's first restaurant *MINT*, in Ranelagh, was awarded a Michelin star in 2008 within 18 months of opening. In his restaurants, Dylan prides himself on offering something for everyone, with innovation, choice, value and consistency at the fore, without the formality of fine dining he was accustomed to. Dylan has also been the subject of many RTE documentaries and programmes, mostly recognised for his role as the judge and presenter on RTE's *MasterChef Ireland*.

CLODAGH MCKENNA is a well known chef, writer and television presenter. She has developed her brand into an emerging business empire which includes *Clodagh's Kitchen* restaurants (Arnotts and Blackrock in Dublin), her television shows, cookbooks and her association with Aer Lingus and their on-board menu. Her hugely popular US TV show, *Clodagh's Irish Food Trails* has been seen by 15 million people. She has recently launched a daily magazine-style food blog, *Clodagh's Daily Digest*.

SALLY MCKENNA is one half of the team that publish the *McKennas' Guides*. Working with her husband, John McKenna, the guides include books, apps, an internet magazine and a website. In 2013 Sally wrote and published *Extreme Greens: Understanding Seaweed*, described by Joanna Blythman as "fascinating, highly informative, extremely digestible and intriguing [a book] that will hold your attention from page one."

JESS MURPHY is Head Chef at Kai in Galway. Originally from New Zealand, Jess made Ireland her home working for Kevin Thornton, the Michelin starred chef. She was head chef at Ard Bia in Galway for 4 years, before setting up Kai restaurant along with her husband David. Jessica's ethos is very simple; all produce is fresh, seasonal, local, and where possible, organic. Depending on the seasonal, fresh produce that is delivered by trusted local and artisan suppliers each day, the menu changes. Her passion for local produce has attracted amateur foragers with handpicked blackberries, apples, sea spinach and other wild things. Jess Murphy was voted Chef of the Year by Hotel and Catering Review and Kai recently received a Michelin BIB award.

RORY O'CONNELL trained at *Ballymaloe House* with Myrtle Allen, the grand-dame of Irish country house cooking. In 1985 he founded *Ballymaloe Cookery School* with his sister Darina Allen. His time as a chef included working with Nico Ladenis and Raymond Blanc in the UK and Alice Waters in the US as well as a ten year tenure as head chef at *Ballymaloe House*. Rory was twice awarded the prestigious title of Ireland's Chef of the Year. His first book *Master It – How to Cook Today* won the André Simon award for 2013.

DERVAL O'ROURKE has held the title of World Champion in sprint hurdles and competed for Ireland in three Olympic Games. As both a foodie and fitness fanatic she is passionate about experimenting with healthy, nutritious recipes. In 2014, Derval announced that she was hanging up her spikes for good after 12 amazing years competing at the highest level in world athletics. She lives in Cork with her husband, Olympic sailor Peter O'Leary, and her much-loved dogs, Berlino and Chaz. Her first book *Food For The Fast Lane* will be published in 2014 by Gill and Macmillan.

EUNICE POWER Eunice has run her own business since 2001, primarily providing outside catering and keeping the people of Dungarvan, County Waterford supplied with delicious food through *Country Store*. She has worked in the food business in Ireland, the UK and Switzerland. Eunice's love of food is evident in her hands-on approach to all of her cooking. She works with small food enterprises, helping them to add value and motivating them to get the most from their businesses. Eunice also works with Failte Ireland and Tourism Ireland and is a tutor at the *Tannery Cookery School* in Dungarvan.

NESSA ROBINS trained as a nurse and worked in many different areas of nursing until she had her third child. Staying at home with her children gave her the opportunity to focus on food and she began to teach cookery classes from her kitchen. She started her award-winning food blog, *Nessa's Family Kitchen*, in January 2010. Her first book *Apron Strings - Recipes from a Family Kitchen* was published in May 2013, by New Island Books. Nessa currently writes, photographs and styles her food columns with *Easy Parenting*, the *Westmeath Independent* and *The Farmer's Journal*. She lives with her husband and four children in Moate, Co. Westmeath.

DONAL SKEHAN is a food writer, food photographer and television presenter living in Dublin. Inspired by a family of passionate food lovers who have worked in the food industry for over 60 years, cooking and eating hearty home cooked food has always been a way of life. His television series include *Kitchen Hero* for RTE and *Junior Masterchef* for the BBC. In 2014 Donal launched his own food range, SKOFF, with fresh pies produced by his parents business. He has also created a new Irish food magazine, *FEAST: A Dinner Journal* which celebrates Irish artisan producers.

BIDDY WHITE LENNON has been a full-time freelance journalist for over 30 years, specialising in food, hospitality and tourism. She has published 12 books - 8 of which were about Irish food culture, its history, recipes and ingredients. Biddy was a founder member of the Irish Food Writers Guild and is an active member of Slow Food. She is a well known forager, restaurant awards judge and travel guide assessor. Biddy rose to prominence through her 1970's TV role of Maggie in *The Riordans* and is back on our screens as Ireland's Mary Berry - in *The Great Irish Bake Off*.

ANNUAL SOWING PLANNER

This is a sowing guide that I put together for myself a few years ago so I would know what I should be sowing in the veg patch each month. For lots more help, tips and resources for your growing year, check out **www.giy.ie**

PLEASE DON'T VIEW THIS as a completely comprehensive guide to growing vegetables. It's not – it's a guide that's based on my own tastes and approach and therefore might need some adaptation to suit your own needs. You might notice for example that there are some vegetables that are completely absent from it – that's because I don't grow them for one reason or another (take a bow asparagus and Jerusalem artichokes). On the other hand, if you stick to this guide it will help you grow nearly 40 different types of vegetables each year and that ain't half bad. In our case this is enough to keep a (hungry) family of four in vegetables for up to 9-10 months a year.

There are a few things to mention about this plan:

▪ I do a lot of sowing 'indoors' in pots and module trays for later transplanting in to the soil outside in the veg patch or in the polytunnel. In my case 'indoors' means in the potting shed down the garden. If you don't have a potting shed, your 'indoors' could be a polytunnel or greenhouse or even in the house on a sunny windowsill. It basically means that you are raising seedlings in a covered environment, safe from weather and pests. There are some vegetables that I sow indoors in module trays that most sane people sow direct outside – an example of this is beetroot. I just always find it more successful to plant a hardy seedling in the ground (4-5 weeks after sowing it indoors) rather than sowing a little seed direct in the soil. And besides, I love spending time in my potting shed. The exceptions to this are the following which I always sow direct in the soil: carrots, parsnips, broad beans, garlic, potatoes, peas, onion sets, shallots and dwarf French beans.

▪ I do a lot of sowing from February to August (sometimes in to September if I am lazy in August). Lots of people sow veg pre-Christmas like broad beans, peas, garlic, over-wintering onions - this is important if you are looking to be 100% self-sufficient, particularly in the 'hungry gap' months (April to June).

I don't do this. I've convinced myself that this is because my soil is too wet for winter sowing, but really I just like to take the winter months off.

▪ The foundation for each month's sowing is what I look on broadly as the 'salad sowing' – lettuce, oriental greens, annual spinach and coriander. I sow one or two 8-module trays of each at the start of each month. With a larger sowing of oriental greens in August for winter use, that keeps us going in salad leaves pretty much all year round.

▪ Where you see a number in brackets beside a vegetable, it indicates that the vegetable is sown more than once. This is 'succession sowing' and it's crucial to maintaining a consistent supply of veg rather than having a glut. You will see that there are some vegetables that I sow up to six times in the growing season.

▪ In addition to the twelve 'veg of the month' featured in this book, there are detailed growing guides for all the vegetables outlined here in the Veg Directory on our website. There are also about 30 little 'how-to' video tutorials (about 3 minutes each), which are well worth a watch. **www.giy.ie**.

WHEN	WHAT	WHERE	HOW
FEBRUARY	Tomatoes	Indoors in pots	10 seeds in a 9cm pot, per variety
	Aubergines	Indoors in pots	10 seeds in a 9cm pot, per variety
	Peppers	Indoors in pots	10 seeds in a 9cm pot, per variety
	Broad Beans	Direct outside	5 cm deep, 15 cm apart in rows 45 cm apart
	Garlic	Direct outside	Just below soil surface, 20 cm apart in rows 25 cm apart
MARCH EARLY	Lettuce (1)	Indoors in module trays	1 seed per module
	Oriental Salads (1)	Indoors in module trays	4-5 seeds per module
	Annual Spinach (1)	Indoors in module trays	3-4 seeds per module
	Coriander (1)	Indoors in module trays	4-5 seeds per module
MARCH LATE	Potatoes (early)	Direct outside	15 cm deep, 25 cm apart in rows 45 cm apart
	Celeriac	Indoors in module trays	2 seeds per module and then thin to one seedling
	Celery (1)	Indoors in module trays	2 seeds per module and then thin to one seedling
	Leeks (1)	Indoors in module trays	2 seeds per module
	Calabrese (1)	Indoors in module trays	1 seed per module
	Cauliflower (1)	Indoors in module trays	1 seed per module
	Scallions (1)	Indoors in module trays	8-10 seeds per module
APRIL EARLY	Lettuce (2)	Indoors in module trays	1 seed per module
	Oriental Salads (2)	Indoors in module trays	4-5 seeds per module
	Annual Spinach (2)	Indoors in module trays	3-4 seeds per module
	Coriander (2)	Indoors in module trays	4-5 seeds per module
	Peas (1)	Direct outside	In a trench 15 cm wide and 4cm deep, sow peas 5cm apart
	Onion Sets	Direct outside	10cm apart in rows 25cm apart
	Shallots	Direct outside	25cm apart in rows 30cm apart
	Cabbage (summer)	Indoors in module trays	1 seed per module
	Kohlrabi (1)	Indoors in module trays	1 seed per module
	Brussels Sprouts (1)	Indoors in module trays	1 seed per module
APRIL LATE	Beetroot (1)	Indoors in module trays	1 seed per module
	Celery (2)	Indoors in module trays	2 seeds per module and then thin to one seedling
	Courgette	Indoors in 7cm pots	1 seed per pot
	Kale (1)	Indoors in module trays	1 seed per module
	Perpetual Spinach (1)	Indoors in module trays	1 seed per module
	Swede (1)	Indoors in module trays	1 seed per module
	Swiss Chard (1)	Indoors in module trays	1 seed per module
	Potatoes (Main Crop)	Direct outside	15cm deep, 35cm apart in rows 70cm apart

WHEN	WHAT	WHERE	HOW
MAY EARLY	Lettuce (3)	Indoors in module trays	1 seed per module
	Oriental Salads (3)	Indoors in module trays	4-5 seeds per module
	Annual Spinach (3)	Indoors in module trays	3-4 seeds per module
	Coriander (3)	Indoors in module trays	4-5 seeds per module
	Sweetcorn	Indoors in module trays	1 seed per module
	Cucumber	Indoors in 7cm pots	1 seed per pot
	Parsnips	Direct outside	2cm deep, 5cm apart in rows 30cm apart (then thin to 10cm)
	Leeks (2)	Indoors in module trays	2 seeds per module
	Calabrese (2)	Indoors in module trays	1 seed per module
	Cauliflower (2)	Indoors in module trays	1 seed per module
	Kohlrabi (2)	Indoors in module trays	1 seed per module
	Squash	Indoors in 7cm pots	1 seed per pot
	Pumpkin	Indoors in 7cm pots	1 seed per pot
	Brussels Sprouts (2)	Indoors in module trays	1 seed per module
MAY LATE	Carrots	Direct outside	thinly, 2cm deep in rows 20cm (then thin to 5cm)
	Climbing French Bean	Indoors in 9cm pots	5cm deep, sow 4-5 seeds per pot
	Dwarf French Bean	Direct outside	5cm deep, 15cm apart in rows 40cm apart
	Runner Bean	Indoors in 9cm pots	5cm deep, sow 4-5 seeds per pot
	Fennel (1)	Indoors in module trays	2 seeds per module and then thin to one seed.
	Peas (2)	Direct outside	In a trench 15 cm wide and 4cm deep, sow peas 5cm apart.
	Beetroot (2)	Indoors in module trays	2 seeds per module and then thin to leave 1 seedling
	Celery (3)	Indoors in pots	2 seeds per module and then thin to one seedling.
	Swede (2)	Indoors in module trays	1 seed per module

Left: *My little corner of heaven in Dunmore East.*

  Annual sowing planner

WHEN	WHAT	WHERE	HOW
JUNE EARLY	Lettuce (4)	Indoors in module trays	1 seed per module
	Oriental Salads (4)	Indoors in module trays	4-5 seeds per module
	Annual Spinach (4)	Indoors in module trays	3-4 seeds per module
	Coriander (4)	Indoors in module trays	4-5 seeds per module
	Calabrese (3)	Indoors in module trays	1 seed per module
	Cauliflower (3)	Indoors in module trays	1 seed per module
	Cabbage (Winter)	Indoors in module trays	1 seed per module
	Fennel (2)	Indoors in module trays	2 seeds per module and then thin to one seed
	Kale (2)	Indoors in module trays	1 seed per module
	Perpetual Spinach (2)	Indoors in module trays	1 seed per module
	Swiss Chard (2)	Indoors in module trays	1 seed per module
JUNE LATE	Purple Sprouting Broccoli	Indoors in module trays	1 seed per module
	Fennel (3)	Indoors in module trays	2 seeds per module and then thin to one seed.
	Kohlrabi (3)	Indoors in module trays	1 seed per module
	Scallions (2)	Indoors in module trays	8-10 seeds per module
JULY	Lettuce (5)	Indoors in module trays	1 seed per module
	Oriental Salads (5)	Indoors in module trays	4-5 seeds per module
	Annual Spinach (5)	Indoors in module trays	3-4 seeds per module
	Coriander (5)	Indoors in module trays	4-5 seeds per module
	Cabbage (Spring)	Indoors in module trays	1 seed per module
AUGUST	Lettuce (6)	Indoors in module trays	1 seed per module
	Oriental Salads (6)	Indoors in module trays	4-5 seeds per module
	Annual Spinach (6)	Indoors in module trays	3-4 seeds per module
	Coriander (6)	Indoors in module trays	4-5 seeds per module

VEGETABLES OF THE MONTH

The downside to picking a veg of the month to appear in a book is that there are far more vegetables than there are months – and so, it becomes an issue of shortlisting and picking favourites which is never a comfortable place to be. I found picking the twelve vegetables of the month to be a little like being asked to pick a favourite child.

Once I had picked the chosen twelve, I immediately felt bad for all the amazing veg that had to be omitted in this most arbitrary of processes – kale, turnip, broad beans, squash, calabrese, sweetcorn and so on. I can only hope the excluded veg don't extract some sort of karmic revenge on me by refusing to grow in the years ahead.

After going through that trauma, I then had to decide what vegetable to put with what month? So for example, if I say potatoes, which month do you think of? March might come to mind, because that's when you plant them? Or maybe May when you harvest the first new potatoes of the season? What about tomatoes? Some people might associate tomatoes with high summer. But for others, February might be 'tomato month' because that's when you start sowing the plants to get them started.

The point is that this is of course an entirely subjective process, and so the best that I can promise is that the twelve chosen vegetables, and their associated month, made sense to me at some point. You will find details on how to grow each vegetable in its appointed month – parsnips in January, leeks in February and so on – as well as relevant recipes.

I've always felt that growing your own food is the very best way to improve your health and the health of your family. Overleaf you will find some notes on the health benefits of each of the twelve vegetables from our good friend, nutritionist Dorcas Barry.

January - Parsnip

The lovely sweet flavour in this root vegetable is due to a type of sugar called inulin, which is a powerful prebiotic. Vegetables containing high levels of prebiotics are essential for feeding the good bacteria in the gut. Parsnips also contain good levels of vitamins B, C and E and are high in fibre, aiding digestion in the body.

February - Leek

Along with onions and garlic, leeks contain high levels of prebiotics, essential for feeding good bacteria in the gut and improving the effectiveness of the digestive system. As a member of the Allium family of vegetables they also contain high levels of sulphur-based compounds, which are beneficial for keeping cholesterol levels low.

March - Cabbage

Cabbage is loaded with vitamin C which is known to protect the body from many diseases and is an important anti-oxidant. Red cabbage boasts even more nutrient content with its high levels of the powerful anti-oxidant, anthocyanin, which is also the reason for the deep rich colour. The anti-oxidant levels in cabbage are also thought to have strong anti-cancer properties which, along with additional anti-inflammatory qualities, make cabbage a superstar vegetable.

April - Lettuce

All greens contain superfood levels of nutrients, and lettuce and salad leaves are serious contenders, containing valuable levels of vitamins, minerals and trace elements. What makes lettuce and salad greens so beneficial is that we eat them raw and so get the maximum nutrient impact that they have to offer, especially when we cut and eat them immediately.

May - Potatoes

Potatoes are by far the best choice when it comes to carbohydrates as they contain vitamin C, unlike other choices such as pasta or white rice. Any new or thin skinned potatoes contain even higher levels of vitamin C and offer higher levels of fibre if the skin is eaten. They also contain some B vitamins, essential for healthy blood and a well functioning nervous system.

June - Peas

Peas are a fantastic source of vitamin C and are generally high in minerals such as potassium. Peas are also a great source of protein as they are classed as pulses as well as vegetables, and also high in soluble fibre for good digestive health and to slow down the absorption of sugar into the bloodstream.

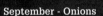

July - Courgettes

This lovely summer vegetable is a great source of heart-friendly potassium, along with other important minerals, and also contains levels of vitamin C. Courgettes are one of the very low calorie vegetables with only 17 calories per 100g and also contain lots of soluble fibre for a super healthy digestive system.

August - Tomatoes

Tomatoes are packed with vitamin C and lycopene, both of which are highly effective anti-oxidants. Anti-oxidants protect the body from cell damage and so can contribute to anti-aging, inside and out. Lycopene, the red colour in tomatoes, helps combat cell damage and is protective against heart disease. The riper and more colourful the tomato, the more lycopene it will contain.

September - Onions

Onions contain high levels of a compound called quercetin, which can have a mild anti-histamine effect in the body, so great for anyone with allergies. They also contain compounds which can reduce inflammation in the body and pack an additional nutritional punch with high levels of inulin, which is an important prebiotic essential for healthy gut health.

October - Beetroot

The intense gorgeous red pigment in beetroot shows that this amazing vegetable is loaded with powerful anti-oxidants, which can have a beneficial effect on liver function by increasing its ability to detoxify the body. The particular anti-oxidants in beetroot (and blueberries) are also fantastic blood builders, can contribute to healthy brain function and boost your memory.

November - Carrots

The wonderful orange colour in carrots is due to the anti-oxidant beta carotene, which converts to vitamin A in the body. Carrots are also rich sources of vitamin C and E, all-important nutrients in protecting against many diseases. Try to eat your carrots with the skin on and only lightly scrubbed as most of their valuable nutrients lie just underneath the skin.

December - Garlic

Garlic is a powerful blood cleanser due to a compound it contains called ajoene, which is very effective in regulating blood clotting. Garlic is also loaded with lots of strong essential oils, responsible for the pungent smell, which can only be removed from the body through the breath. In this process the essential oils move through the respiratory system, killing off bugs and viruses and offering protection from colds and flu.

January

EVERY YEAR I WORRY A LITTLE about whether I will find enthusiasm for growing my own food again – what if the year turns and I am not motivated any more?

I always take a decent break from the veg patch in December – it's the one month when there's very little work to do and the garden will forgive you if you don't show up. You're in wind down mode, the run in to Christmas and end of year. The GIY "to-do" list is always full of things that no sensible person really bothers with – like cleaning your spade and mending fences and the like. But then BOOM, the clock moves over New Year's Eve and in to New Year's Day, and you wake up bleary eyed in to a new year and a new growing season beckons. How did that happen?

Of course, though it's the start of the new year, it's still winter. The days are short and cold, and the garden is generally uninviting. Little wonder then that my enthusiasm for GIYing generally doesn't show up until either February (when I can start sowing some seeds) or March (when you can practically smell growth in the air). If you're of a mind for it, there are things you could be doing outside. At the very least get your seeds ordered and get yourself ready!

THIS MONTH'S TOP JOBS

* Spread well rotted compost or manure on veggie beds.

* Start a compost heap.

* Order seeds, seed potatoes, garlic and onion sets.

* Join a GIY group!

Things to Do in... *January*

PREPARATION

If you haven't already done so, you could still spread some manure or compost on your vegetable and fruit beds and cover them down with black polythene to start warming them up for spring sowing. Make sure that it's well-rotted manure and be careful not to spread fresh manure in beds which will take root vegetables in late spring. If you don't have a compost heap, this is a good time of the year to get one started. Timber pallets are a cheap and easy way to build a heap for all your garden waste. Consider a compost trench for your legume (peas and beans) bed – bury kitchen waste at a spade's depth and cover with soil.

TO DO LIST

If you have any root vegetables left in the soil, it's probably a good idea to get them out of there now as January-March are months when you get very heavy frosts and inclement weather – so lift anything that might still be in the soil such as parsnips, carrots and celeriac. Cover down bare beds with mulch, leaves, compost or polythene. Rhubarb is typically the first fresh crop of the spring, particularly if you "force" it now by covering it to exclude any light. Put a layer of straw on top of the dormant plants and then cover with an upturned pot. Tender little stems should be ready to eat in March. January is also a good month to split the rhubarb plants if you want to propagate. Get organised: start collecting old plastic bottles and containers as cloches and covers, and collect toilet roll inserts to use as pots for sowing. Order your seeds and seed potatoes.

SOWING SEEDS AND PLANTING OUT

Don't be tempted to sow seeds too early. Be patient – it won't be long.

Right: *The veg patch blanketed in winter snow.*

HARVESTING – WHAT'S IN SEASON?

Though things are bleak in the garden, ironically you might have plenty of good things to eat fresh from the garden and from your 'larder' courtesy of last year's growing. Outside in the veg patch harvest perpetual spinach, chard, leeks and kale, all of which are very good to eat. You may also have winter cabbage, cauliflowers and some Brussels sprouts left in the ground if you didn't eat them all during Christmas. Depending on how successful your growing/ storage regime last year was, you may well still be tucking in to stores of potatoes, celeriac, carrots, parsnips, onions, jerusalem artichokes, winter squash, pumpkins and beetroot. It's also possible to have winter salads like land cress, corn salad and mizuna at this time of the year, particularly in a polytunnel or greenhouse.

Left: *Carrot crop for winter storage.*

Veg of the Month - *Parsnips*

WHY GROW THEM?

Earthy and homely, parsnips really do provide the quintessential taste of winter. Worth growing just for the smell you get when you pluck a parsnip from the soil on a cold winter's day. Unlike carrots, they are relatively easy to grow (once you have persuaded them to germinate), needing very little attention. They will also stay in the ground quite happily until you're ready to eat them.

SOWING

Dig bed deeply in winter but do not manure (causes forking in roots). Break down clods, rake well and add an organic fertiliser a week before sowing. Most parsnip seed packets will tell you to sow them in February - don't do it. Far better to leave it until late April or early May. The seeds won't germinate in cold, wet soil and later-sown parsnips are less likely to get canker.

   Make a drill 2cm deep – if soil is dry, dampen. Sow seeds every 5cm in rows 30cm apart and cover in with soil. Germination takes up to three weeks. When they germinate, thin to 10cm spacing which will produce medium sized roots.

   How many to sow? Depends on how many parsnips you like to eat! Because they store well, I think they are a useful crop to have around in the winter months, so I grow about 70, which will provide roughly 3 a week between November and April. In a standard bed you will get three rows of parsnips - if you space the parsnips at 10cm in each row you will get 30 parsnips per meter, so you will need a bed 2.5m long to get 75 parsnips.

GROWING

Very little maintenance needed. Weed carefully until well established. Watering shouldn't be necessary except in dry spells.

HARVESTING

Parsnips are ready to rock when the foliage starts to die away in autumn but flavour improves after the first frosts. You can leave them in the soil until you are ready to eat them, but lift by February. Lift carefully with a fork.

GIY RECOMMENDED VARIETIES

Javelin, Tender and True, Gladiator.

PROBLEMS

Canker (a fungus that produces brown/black growths on roots) is the main issue. Avoid sowing too early and use canker resistant varieties. Occasionally, carrot root fly can be a problem.

GIY TIPS

▪ Always use fresh (this years) seed – parsnip seeds don't store well.
▪ Try sowing seed in toilet roll inserts filled with compost. Once seedling is established, pop the whole insert in to a hole in the ground. Works a treat!

MONTHLY INSIGHT– GETTING STARTED

If you're anything like me, when you make a decision to grow your own food you will probably want to grow ALL your own food. Fight that temptation. No matter how fired up you are, it's never a good idea to dig up your entire garden or to make a commitment to becoming 100% self-sufficient in year 1. Growing your own food is a skill – a proper, genuine life skill – and like any skill worth having, it takes time to cultivate it. So, be patient. Give your expertise time to catch up with your enthusiasm! If I was to give one piece of advice to people starting off on their growing journey, it would be summed up in these two words: start small! The worst thing you could possibly do is over reach at this early stage – you will almost certainly end up with a veg patch full of weeds and a whole load of guilt and heartache.

DECIDING WHAT TO GROW

Make a list of what you would like to grow. Deciding what you will grow is typically a factor of the following:

- How much space do you have? In a space-constrained garden or apartment balcony you probably won't want to be growing globe artichokes (big plant, little food). Focus instead on vegetables that give a high return for a small amount of space, like beetroot or carrots.
- How much time do you have? Some vegetables are very easy to grow, requiring little maintenance (say parsnips for example) while others require regular attention (like tomatoes). Think about your lifestyle – can you spend a few hours on a Saturday in the veg patch or do you have to ferry children around to various activities? I reckon on average about 3-4 hours per week is required to keep yourself and your family in veg all year round.
- What do you like to eat? It sounds obvious but seriously, don't grow things you don't like to eat.
- If you're time-constrained, think about the cost of food (though that's not always the reason why people GIY) – some vegetables are so cheap you might be as well to buy them and focus your efforts on more costly vegetables.

DECIDING WHERE TO GROW

For many of us, the location of the deck, the garage, the patio, the kid's slide etc., dictates where our veg patch will go. But if you have options it's worth investing some time in this decision. Bear in mind the following:

- Pick the sunniest position possible – some veg will grow in shade or semi-shade, but they are in the minority. The rest are sun worshippers – a bit like ourselves I guess.
- Steer clear of large hedges and trees – they will send out roots in to the lovely soil in your veg beds or cast shade over them, or both. Neither is good for your veggies.
- A sheltered spot is preferable – a windswept veg patch is never a good plan.
- Be near a water supply for easy watering or invest in a long hose!
- Soil quality – obviously it would be nice if you could position your veg patch where there is great soil, but this is seldom possible. And besides, take it from someone whose garden is positioned on a bog – any soil can be improved over time with some raised beds and yearly applications of compost.

JANUARY TIPS

SORT YOUR SEEDS

Check through your seed packets and discard any veg seeds that are out of date. You might think, 'ah sure I will hold on to them, they might work'. It's not worth it! There is nothing more frustrating than going to the trouble of sowing seeds and then finding they haven't germinated because the seed is out of date – you are basically delaying the point at which you have food to eat by 2-3 weeks!

DON'T TREAD ON ME!

Be careful not to get too enthusiastic about preparing soil at this time of the year. If you work on soil when it's wet, it will damage the soil structure. If the soil sticks to your boots when you walk on it, then you shouldn't be walking on it. If you have to walk on the soil to get at your veggies, put a plank of timber down and walk on that instead. The timber distributes your weight more evenly. If you haven't already done so, it's worth covering down an area of your soil to warm it up for the spring – use a cloche or black polythene. This will make the soil warm up far quicker than it would otherwise and will mean you can start sowing in it far earlier. In very wet weather it will also help to dry the soil out.

TIPS FOR GROWING GOOD CARROTS

One of the most common problems that people have with carrots is that they end up with stumped or forked roots – now, though the first couple might be fun to look at (particularly if they're rude looking), after that it is just plain annoying. There are three main causes here: (1) Forking of roots occurs if there are stones in the soil or if the soil is very compacted. I mainly practice 'no-dig' GIYing, but I do dig the carrot bed thoroughly in springtime to make sure the soil is in good nick to a spade's depth and that any large stones are removed. (2) Forking can also be caused by too much fresh manure or compost being added to the soil in spring. The root will literally fork off in search of a pocket of nutrients rather than growing down. If you need to feed the soil in your carrot bed, do so in the autumn. Finally (3), carrots don't transplant well and any disturbance to the seedling when you're transplanting can cause forked roots. So, it's always better to sow carrot seeds direct in the soil.

NO BUTTS?

It is estimated that around 24,000 litres of rain water can be saved from the average house roof every year. Most water butts will hold between 200 and 350 litres of rain - that's a lot of water! So, a water butt is a great investment and depending on the size of your veg patch (and the amount of rainfall) you may not need a hose at all. Find a suitable down pipe, and attach the water butt to it - try and make sure the water butt is near your vegetable patch. Several water butts can be "daisy-chained" together to maximise the amount of water being saved.

Gratin of Parsnips and Jerusalem Artichokes

RACHEL ALLEN

This is a delicious vegetarian Christmas dish, served with some red cabbage and roast potatoes. It is also very good with roast duck – or with turkey too, for that matter.

SERVES 6

500g (17 ½ oz) parsnips, peeled and sliced ½ cm (¼ in) thick

500g (17 ½ oz) Jerusalem artichokes, peeled and sliced ½ cm (¼in) thick

10g (½ oz) butter, for greasing the dish

salt and pepper

250ml (8 ¾ fl oz) cream

100 ml (3 ½ fl oz) milk

1 tbsp wholegrain mustard

75g (3oz) grated Gruyère or Parmesan cheese

5 sprigs thyme

From *Rachel's Favourite Food for Friends* by Rachel Allen. Gill and MacMillan, 2005.

Preheat the oven to 200°C/400°F/gas 6. In a saucepan of boiling water with a pinch of salt, blanch the parsnip slices for about 4-5 minutes until just soft. Pull out the parsnips and put in the Jerusalem artichoke slices and blanch these till soft. Drain. Butter an ovenproof dish (30cm x 20cm (12in x 8in) and in it place the blanched vegetables, arranging them slightly. Season with salt and pepper. In a saucepan, place the cream, milk and mustard. Bring to just under boiling point and pour the mixture over the parsnips and artichokes. The liquid should half cover the vegetables. Sprinkle with the grated cheese, and pop the sprigs of thyme on top. The dish can be prepared in advance to this point. Cook in the preheated oven for 25-35 minutes or until it is golden and bubbly. You can cover it with tin foil for the last 10 minutes or so if it is already brown enough.

NOTE If preparing the artichokes a few minutes in advance, store them in a bowl of water with a squeeze of lemon juice – otherwise, they go brown very quickly.

Spiced Butternut Squash and Coconut soup

CLODAGH MCKENNA

This combination works so well together. If you are not a fan of coconut milk then just replace with vegetable or chicken stock and try adding a little chorizo.

SERVES 4

20g butter

1kg butternut squash, skinned, deseeded and cut into 2.5 cm pieces

1 teaspoon ground cumin

1 teaspoon garam masala

2 garlic cloves, crushed

200g onions, chopped

700ml hot vegetable stock

300ml coconut milk

sea salt and freshly ground black pepper

From *Clodagh's Kitchen Diaries* by Clodagh McKenna. Published by Kyle Books 2012.

Melt the butter in a heavy-bottomed saucepan, add the squash, spices, garlic and onions and season with salt and pepper. Cover and leave to simmer, stirring occasionally, for about 15 minutes.

Stir in the stock and coconut milk and bring the soup to the boil. When the squash is tender the soup is ready to be blended using a food-processor or hand blender. Serve hot.

Raw Kale Salad

DORCAS BARRY

The massaging action of the lemon juice and salt into the kale in this recipe softens it, almost "cooking" the leaves making them much more palatable while still retaining all of the nutrients contained in the raw green leaves. Adding the pine nuts and cranberries provides colour and texture, but you could add any extra ingredients you like to the kale, depending on your taste. This salad keeps for up to three days in the fridge and is a great way to make sure you are eating enough greens throughout the winter.

SERVES 2-4

250g kale

juice of 1 lemon

25g dried cranberries (chopped finely)

25g pine nuts, roasted

4-5 spring onions, chopped finely

2-3 stalks of celery, chopped finely

olive oil

salt and pepper

From Dorcas Barry www.dorcasbarry.com

Remove the stalks from the kale and roll each leaf before chopping into fine strips.

Place into a large bowl, add the lemon juice and 2-3 pinches of sea salt. Massage the juice and salt into the kale using your fingers until it starts to soften slightly, making sure that all the leaves are coated and the oil and salt are well worked in. Sprinkle with olive oil and leave to sit for 10 minutes to soften further. Before serving, add the cranberries, pine nuts, celery and spring onions and stir well. Sprinkle more olive oil if needed.

Celeriac and Lemon Thyme Crème Brûlée

MARK DIACONO

There ought to be a custodial sentence for messing with the traditional crème brûlée, but mess with it I have. Celeriac and lemon thyme sounds an unlikely combination for a brûlée, but it is, I promise, really very fine. If you haven't any lemon thyme, lemon Verbena works perfectly well, or you can substitute a couple of sprigs of regular thyme with some finely grated lemon zest. When I made the brûlée opposite, I had an accident that turned into a happy one: the blowtorch used to finish the brûlées ran out of gas on the last one and turned out, as in the picture, partly topped in hot sugar, with islands of solid caramel. It suited the celeriac perfectly.

SERVES 6

370g celeriac

50g butter

120ml milk

8 free-range egg yolks

140g caster sugar

500ml double cream

1½ vanilla pods

8 or so sprigs of lemon thyme

120g soft light brown sugar

From *A Year at Otter Farm* by Mark Diacono, Bloomsbury 2014.

Peel and chop the celeriac into pieces about the size of a pound coin. Melt the butter in a pan over a medium heat and add the celeriac. Cook over a low heat for about 10 minutes until the celeriac begins to soften. Add the milk and simmer until the celeriac is tender, about 15-20 minutes. Purée the mixture in a blender until smooth.

Preheat the oven to 150°C/Gas 2.

Whisk the egg yolks and sugar together in a large bowl until pale and creamy. Pour the cream into a pan. Split the vanilla pods lengthways, tease out the seeds and add them and the pods to the cream, along with the lemon thyme. Bring just to the boil, then strain the hot cream through a sieve onto the egg and sugar mix, discarding the vanilla pods and thyme. Whisk briefly, then add the celeriac purée and whisk to combine.

Stand 6 ramekins in a roasting tin and fill them with the custard. Pour enough boiling water into the tin to come two-thirds of the way up the side of the ramekins. Cover the tin loosely with foil. Cook for 20-25 minutes, until the custard is just set - it should have a little wobble to it.

Lift the ramekins out of the water and leave the custards to cool, then refrigerate for at least a couple of hours or overnight.

Sprinkle each brûlée with 4 tsp sugar and caramelise with a kitchen blowtorch. If you don't have a blowtorch, use a very hot grill.

February

THOUGH ST. BRIGID'S DAY (Feb 1st) is considered the start of spring in the Celtic Calendar, it's really still winter outside in the veggie patch. Come February 1st I am always itching to get started with my seed sowing and of course you can get lots of vegetables started in seed trays on a sunny windowsill indoors at this time of the year. The problem is that when they are bursting from their pots and ready to be planted out in a month's time, it may still be too cold to do so.

The relative lack of light (due to the short days) can also cause problems for seedlings at this time of the year – tiny seedlings literally strain to reach the light and can end up getting too long and 'leggy' as a result. I generally confine myself to sowing tomatoes, aubergines and peppers indoors in the potting shed in February – these vegetables have a long growing season and therefore benefit from early sowing. Outside, I sow my broad beans and garlic. Most people sow garlic pre-Christmas, but my garden is wet and the soil is heavy, so I hold off until spring – besides, it's good to be contrary.

As we move further and further from the winter solstice, we gain about five minutes of daylight at either end of the day, each day, and comparable dollops of optimism. Roll on spring!

THIS MONTH'S TOP JOBS

* Start monthly indoor sowing of lettuce, oriental greens, annual spinach, calabrese, coriander.

* Sow indoors (with heat): tomatoes, aubergines, peppers and beetroot (for early polytunnel crop).

* Sow outdoors: broad beans, garlic.

* Chit seed potatoes.

Things to Do in... *February*

PREPARATION

If you didn't do so earlier in the winter, spread well rotted manure or compost over vegetable beds and cover selected areas with cardboard, black plastic or carpet to start warming up the soil. The soil in raised beds will warm two weeks at least before open ground which will make it easier to grow in later in the spring. For those beds which are not covered, gently prepare the soil if the weather is good (remove any weeds, rake to flat etc.). Keep off the beds to prevent soil compaction - use timber planks to stand on for access. If you have not already done so order/buy your seeds, spuds and onions. Chit seed potatoes – put them in a container (e.g. used egg carton or empty seed tray) and leave them in a bright warm place.

TO DO LIST

Prune fruit trees and bushes if necessary, to improve their shape and remove winter damage to the bushes (it's best to complete this job before spring when the sap begins to rise). Consider netting the bushes after pruning (fruit netting can be bought in DIY stores & garden centres - it's worth it unless you want your fruit to become a nice treat for local birds) and dress the ground around with a potash feed (or use wood ash), which encourages fruit growth. Check the pH of your soil – you can buy a soil pH testing kit in any garden centre or on the GIY webshop. Lime your soil now if it is acid – ground limestone or crushed chalk are the most common forms. The addition of lime is particularly important in your brassica bed. Scrub seed trays with hot soapy water in

Far left, top: *Early spring growth in the potting shed*

Left: Holy chit! *Chitting some of my favourite potato varieties*

preparation for sowing – dirty old seed trays can harbour disease.

SOWING SEEDS AND PLANTING OUT

Finally, we can sow some seeds. On a sunny windowsill indoors, in a heated greenhouse or on a heating mat: sow tomatoes, aubergines, and peppers/chilli-peppers. If you have a polytunnel or greenhouse to plant them out in to later, you could also sow beetroot, lettuce and oriental greens. Outside in the veg patch, sow garlic if you haven't done so before Christmas, and weather permitting sow broad beans. Now is a good time to plant fruit trees and bushes. It's also a great time to start planning a herb garden - get root cuttings of perennial herbs i.e. mint, fennel, thyme etc. from fellow GIYers. Buy seeds for the annual herbs like basil and coriander.

HARVESTING – WHAT'S IN SEASON?

Winter cabbage and cauliflowers, Brussels sprouts, spinach, kale and leeks. You could also still be enjoying 'fresh' vegetables from storage such as potatoes, carrots, celeriac, beetroot and parsnips – check them regularly for rotting or re-sprouting and remove damaged ones.

Veg of the Month - *Leeks*

WHY GROW THEM?

Leeks are quite easy to grow and will withstand even the harshest winter. For many GIYers they are the only crop left in the soil during the winter months. You can grow a decent amount of leeks in a relatively small space. They are another of the classic stockpot vegetables.

SOWING

Leeks are best grown in modules before being transplanted to their final growing position later. They are very easy to grow from seed. Sow one or two seeds per module just 1cm deep (they are a small, black seed). They will take about two weeks to germinate. For a continuous supply of leeks sow as follows: (1) February – plant out in April, will be ready to eat in early autumn. (2) March – plant out in May, will be ready to eat in early winter. (3) May – plant out in June, will be ready to eat in late winter.

GROWING

Leeks are heavy feeders so it's best to grow them in fertile soil that has been enriched with plenty of farmyard manure or compost. Spread a general purpose organic fertiliser before planting out. They will be ready to plant out about 2 months after sowing (when they are pencil size). You can either plant the two leek seedlings from a single module together (to get two smaller leeks), or remove one (to get one larger leek). Leek seedlings seem to be fairly hardy and will withstand some handling.
Some people "puddle in" leeks - that is, they make a deep hole with a dibber, drop the leek in and then fill the hole with water. They do not backfill with soil, instead leaving the hole to fill itself in gradually over the following months. I am not sure about the logic of that approach, and have given it up as a bit of a palaver. These days I just plant leeks like any other seedling (i.e. firming them in well with soil) and it

seems to work fine! Leave 15cm between plants and 30cm between rows. Keep the leek bed well weeded. Leeks have to be earthed up during the growing season – this process encourages the bleaching or whitening of the stem. If you don't earth up you will be left with leeks which are predominantly green with just a small amount of edible white stem. Earth up a few times during the season.

HARVESTING

The best leeks are the small tender ones – they decrease in flavour as they grow larger, so don't aim to produce prize-winning ones. Lift the leek with a fork – their roots are surprisingly fibrous and strong, and you will break the leek if you try to pull it by hand. Winter varieties can stay in the ground until needed, they are practically indestructible – though repeated freezing and re-thawing in winter weather will eventually turn 'em to mush.

GIY RECOMMENDED VARIETIES

Zermatt, Tadorna, Carentan, Giant Winter.

PROBLEMS

Leek rust is an issue – it's an airborne fungus that affects all the allium family, particularly garlic. Though the leeks look unattractive when infected, it doesn't affect the taste at all. You can try cleaning them carefully, but this doesn't work in my experience. Leeks can also get white rot, which is why you should include them in your allium (onion) rotation.

GIY TIPS

- I've heard of GIYers who use kitchen roll inserts to "earth up" leeks – pop the insert over the leek and it does the same job as earthing up. Nice idea.
- Be careful not to get soil in to the heart of the leek when earthing up – this can be a nightmare to get out when cooking.

MONTHLY INSIGHT– COMPOST & MANURE

The natural order of things is that when we eat food, we take nutrients from the food which the plant has taken from the soil. It goes without saying therefore that the soil we eat our food from should be as nutrient rich as possible. Composting is the process of turning plant and animal matter in to a rich, highly nutritious material. By adding this material to our soil, we make our soil more fertile.

When food grows in the veg patch, it takes nutrients from the soil (this means that over time the soil becomes depleted of vital nutrients); the plants then travel the short distance to the compost corner, where, aided by an army of organisms, they rot down and release their nutrients. This composted material is then ferried back to the veg patch to nurture the next season's crops. It's the ultimate closed-loop virtuous system and my health, and the health of my family, relies on it functioning properly.

The most important nutrients that your vegetables require to grow are nitrogen (N), phosphorus (P) and potassium (K). The goal of any fertiliser (organic or artificial) is to make plants grow by supplying these elements in readily available forms. In general the nutrients in fertilisers are important to plants for the following:

N: Nitrogen, for producing leaf growth.
P: Phosphorus, to produce fruit and a strong root system.
K: Potassium (potash), for strength, flower colour and size.

Application Tip: I add a layer of compost about 5cm thick to all of my beds each winter, except the bed which will take root crops the following year (carrots, parsnips etc.). It is generally accepted that adding compost to the root bed can cause 'forking' in carrots and parsnips.

Compost, farmyard manure and seaweed are basically, natural fertilisers. They supply these essential nutrients but also lots of other micro-nutrients. At the same time, they improve soil composition (in a way that chemical fertilisers do not). I can vouch for the fact that you can magically (but gradually) turn a heavy clay soil in to a lovely friable light soil over a number of years by adding compost or manure each winter.

Home-made garden or kitchen compost is rich in NPK so you should try to produce as much of this as you can. Farmyard manure from pigs, sheep, horses, cows or poultry is great, but a little harder to acquire - and must be well-rotted before applying (which generally takes 8-12 months). Seaweed is also amazing, but generally only available to those living by the sea. Home-made liquid fertilizers provide a boost to vegetables during the growing season – these could be: comfrey, which is potash rich; nettle which is rich in nitrogen and potash; and animal manure which has all three nutrients.

It would be nice of course to be completely self-sufficient in compost – to 'close the gate' on your garden's nutrient needs, so to speak, but this mightn't be practical for most people. I generally need to source some well-rotted farmyard manure from a local farmer to supplement the compost I make in the garden.

Right: *The engine room of my veg patch – one of the compost heaps at the end of the garden.*

FEBRUARY TIPS

SOWING TOMATOES, AUBERGINES AND PEPPERS

Though it might seem strange to be sowing what seem like the quintessential summer crops in February, aubergines, peppers and toms have a very long growing season and are therefore generally some of the first seeds to be sown each year. Unfortunately all three require quite high temperatures to germinate (in excess of 20 degrees), which clearly we don't have outside yet. For this reason you will need to sow them indoors in pots/trays in a very sunny, warm room. They will then be planted out in May. Alternatively, if you do your seed sowing in the glasshouse, polytunnel or potting shed you can place the trays or pots on a heating mat (which warms up the soil) or in an electric propagation unit (which warms up the ambient temperature). In my potting shed, I have a heating mat with a thermostat which turns the unit off if it gets too hot by day.

FROSTS

We're still very vulnerable to overnight frosts which will cause havoc for seedlings and plants. Keep an eye on the weather forecast and cover new seedlings with fleece if you think a frost is due (even those sown in a potting shed or polytunnel). You can buy horticultural fleece in most garden centres.

HOE

Learning how to use a hoe properly has been a revelation for me, turning weeding from a real chore to something a little more manageable. I find the key to staying on top of weeds in the veg patch is to hoe little but often. I use an oscillating hoe regularly in the vegetable patch to stop weeds from taking hold - ideally you want to hoe to prevent weeds as opposed to getting rid of them. Hoeing basically dislodges the roots and forces them to die - they then rot down and add to soil fertility. Hoeing is eight times faster than pulling weeds (apparently)! From February to September I try to run over the entire patch with a hoe each week - it's enjoyable work if you do it right, standing upright with a long-handled hoe and moving it forward and back just beneath the soil surface. Hoeing on a sunny day is best, as the weeds will then shrivel up and die. I use a 'Dutch' hoe (with a smaller head) for more precise hoeing (e.g. in between onions).

LIME

Most vegetables prefer to grow in a slightly acid soil with the exception of brassicas which prefer alkaline conditions. Adding compost/manure to soil to improve fertility each year, eventually makes the soil too acidic for most vegetables and particularly for the brassicas. Traditionally therefore GIYers add lime in the spring to the beds where they will plant their brassicas to reduce acidity. Never add manure/compost at the same time as lime, as they react badly together. How much lime to add depends on the type of soil and it's pH value (buy a pH testing kit in any garden centre), but typically 1lb per square yard is about right.

Baby Leek Gratin with Smoked Gubbeen

Smoked Gubbeen has a very distinctive flavour and enhances the béchamel sauce in this recipe.

SERVES 4

1 kg of young leek, cut in 3cm pieces with a tooth pick to keep them whole

25g butter

20g plain flour

300ml milk

100g Smoked Gubbeen, crumbled

salt and pepper

From *Kevin Dundon's Modern Irish Food* by Kevin Dundon. Published by Mitchell Beazley 2013

Preheat the oven to 200°C/400°F/gas mark 6.

Bring a large saucepan of salted water to the boil. Add the leeks and blanch for 3–6 minutes until tender. Remove them with a slotted spoon, drain thoroughly and place in an ovenproof dish. Reserve 200ml (1 cup) of the leek cooking water.

Meanwhile, melt the butter in a saucepan over a medium heat and stir in the flour.

Cook for about 2 minutes until a light golden colour. Pour in the milk and reserved water and whisk vigorously until smooth.

Bring to a simmer and cook for 8–10 minutes. Remove from the heat and add the cheese, stirring until melted.

Pour the sauce over the leeks and season with salt and black pepper. Place the dish in the oven and bake for 5 minutes until caramelized.

Vichyssoise

TRISH DESEINE

This famous and much loved French soup is a rather formal but tasty starter whose ingredients can be picked up fresh from the market all year round. If you announce to a French greengrocer that you are making stock, he will put together a collection of vegetables for you. As leeks are so flavoursome, you could save yourself the trouble of making your own stock and just use water and leeks for this recipe. But it's hard not to be tempted when you're faced with the choice, quality and facility of today's vegetable market stand. I quite like my Vichyssoise warm so that's what I am suggesting in this recipe, though it is traditionally served chilled. If you like it cold, replace the butter with olive oil when you sweat the leeks.

SERVES 4

50g butter

2 leeks, thoroughly rinsed and chopped

300g potatoes, peeled and chopped

1 litre vegetable stock

salt and freshly ground black pepper

double cream (optional)

chopped fresh chervil, tarragon and/or parsley

From *Trish's French Kitchen* by Trish Deseine, published by Kyle Books, 2008.

Heat the butter in a saucepan and sweat the leeks without colouring. Add the potatoes, give things a good stir and cook for several minutes.

Pour in the stock and bring to the boil. Leave to simmer for about 10 minutes, until the vegetables are soft.

Blitz in a blender, season with salt and pepper and add more stock or water if the soup seems too thick.

You could add a little cream if you like before serving, garnished with the fresh herbs.

Potato and Jerusalem Artichoke Soup

This is very rich. I used oyster mushrooms but you can use any mushrooms you like. Porcini would be fabulous, but Portobellos will do. If you have it, add a few drops of truffle oil at the end.

SERVES 4-6

5 large potatoes, peeled and chopped

500g Jerusalem artichokes, peeled

3 cloves garlic, peeled

60g butter

250ml cream

250ml milk

salt and freshly ground black pepper

200g mushrooms, thinly sliced

chopped fresh parsley, to garnish

Parmesan shavings, to garnish

From *itsa Cookbook* by Domini Kemp.
Published by Gill & Macmillan Ltd 2010

Put the spuds, artichokes and garlic in a large saucepan and fill with cold water. Bring to the boil and simmer till the spuds are practically disintegrating. Drain and put back in the saucepan with half the butter. Add the cream and milk and gently heat up.

I then blitzed this in a blender, and because the spuds were cooked to hell, I reckon most of the starch was long gone, hence the soup didn't go all goey. Put the mixture back in the saucepan and heat until just simmering. Season well. (You can either serve it now or let it cool down fully and reheat before serving.) If it's too thick, add more milk or cream but make sure you season it again.

Fry the mushrooms on a high heat in the remaining butter and season well. Serve the soup with mushrooms on top, then garnish with some parsley, Parmesan and a few drops of good olive or truffle oil.

Brussels Sprouts with Spiced Potato Gnocchi and Roast Shallots in a Blue Cheese Cream

DENIS COTTER

SERVES 4

400g floury potatoes

60g hard cheese

2 egg yolks

½ tsp cayenne pepper

80g plain flour

200g small shallots, peeled

400g Brussels sprouts

4 cloves garlic, chopped

¼ teaspoon caraway seeds

150mls vegetable stock or water

300mls cream

80g blue cheese

olive oil

knob of butter

nutmeg to serve

From *wild garlic, gooseberries…and me.* Published by Collins 2010.

Peel and steam the potatoes, then gently mash them and leave them to cool in a bowl. Stir in the cheese, egg yolks and cayenne, then quickly work in most of the flour. Season well with salt and pepper. If the dough seems firm enough, cut off a small piece, roll it into a ball and drop it into boiling water. If, after a few minutes, the ball floats without breaking up, the dough has enough flour. Bear in mind that the flour helps the gnocchi to hold together but too much flour can make the dough tough. Cut the dough in three and roll each piece with your hands to form a tube 2cm thick. Cut these into pieces 1cm long and shape each piece into an elongated ball. Keep these on a lightly floured plate as you go.

Toss the shallots in a little olive oil in an oven dish, cover loosely with parchment and roast in a medium oven, checking and stirring occasionally, until the shallots are soft and coloured.

Halve or quarter the Brussels sprouts, depending on size. In a wide pan, heat a tablespoon of butter and cook the sprouts, garlic and caraway for three minutes. Add the stock or water, bring it to a boil, cover and simmer for five minutes, until the sprouts are almost tender. Add the cream and boil it for 30 seconds, then crumble in the blue cheese. Turn off the heat and stir to melt the cheese.

While the sprouts are cooking, bring a pot of water to a boil and drop in some of the gnocchi, being careful not to overcrowd the pot and causing the gnocchi to stick together. As the gnocchi float to the top, remove them with a slotted spoon. Keep them warm in a little butter in a frying pan over low heat while you cook the rest.

To serve, place some gnocchi in four warm plates or shallow bowls. Spoon the sprouts in their sauce around each portion, pouring some of the sauce over the gnocchi. Arrange some roasted shallots over each portion and finish with nutmeg.

March

MARCH IS OFFICIALLY THE FIRST month of spring. Hurrah! It is a key month in the food grower's garden and the first of three exceptionally busy months for the GIYer. Though the weather can still be problematic, spring is very much in the air. The sap is rising in plants, and perhaps in us GIYers too. On the downside, the grass needs cutting.

After the 'phoney war' that was February, there's plenty of seed sowing to be done in the potting shed with seeds to be sown for later transplanting outside. Significantly, this month we really get stuck in to outdoor sowings too, most notably of potatoes around St Patrick's Day.

Generally speaking in March I am also starting to give my veg beds some attention - clearing those that need clearing, taking the covers off others and forking over those that will take crops in the coming months. Above all, I'm enjoying being out in the veg patch again after the long winter months and when the sun shines, it warms the soul.

Though it's sort of on life support now, last year's GIYing is still bearing fruit with leeks and purple sprouting broccoli still in full swing from the veg patch and the larder still throwing up the occasional nugget. By the way, it's still not too late to get a vegetable patch ready if you are just starting out this year. I always say to people that you could build and fill a raised bed in a few hours, and plant veg in it the next day, so don't delay!

THIS MONTH'S TOP JOBS

* Monthly indoor sowing of lettuce, oriental greens, annual spinach, calabrese, coriander.

* Sow indoors: celeriac, celery, leeks, cauliflower, scallions.

* Sow outdoors: early potatoes.

* Start slug patrols – show no mercy to those critters that would eat your seedlings!

* Keep on top of new season weeds.

Things to Do in... March

PREP WORK

Continue to prepare ground – there is still time to prepare a plot or make a raised bed to grow vegetables this summer. Remove the covering from covered beds that will need to be used for planting in March. Fork or rake over the soil and break up large clods of earth. Avoid treading on the soil. In mild weather you can start to harden off hardier seedlings by moving them outside during the day. Don't forget to bring them back in at night. Don't be fooled by the slight warmth in the air - March can still bring heavy frosts which will cause havoc for some seedlings and plants, such as potato plants. Keep an eye on the weather forecast and cover new seeds with fleece if you think a frost is due. You can buy horticultural fleece in most garden centres.

Sowing potatoes with my little helper

TO DO LIST

Once you sow seeds or seedlings in the green house, polytunnel or outside you need to protect them from your nemesis, the slug. Start your daily slug patrols and lay beer traps. Don't let new-season weeds take over your plot – now's the time to get on top of them by hoeing. Hoe your entire veggie patch once a week if possible. This is the last chance to prune apple trees and perennial herb plants like thyme and mint etc. Top dress over-wintered crops such as onions, spring cabbage etc. Use good quality compost or well rotted chicken manure – this will give the crops a good spring boost.

SEEDS TO SOW

Sow indoors on a sunny windowsill or in a heated greenhouse: lettuce, oriental salads, spinach, celeriac, leeks, calabrese, cauliflower, scallions and celery. Outdoors, plant your first early

seed potatoes, as soon as weather conditions allow – St. Patrick's Day traditionally but wait until the soil is warm and weather has improved. If you are so inclined, plant asparagus crowns, globe artichokes and Jerusalem artichoke tubers. It's worth growing the following flowers because of the benefits they bring to your veggies: calendula (marigold), centaurea (cornflower) and nasturtium. These pretty annuals will help deter aphids and whitefly while attracting beneficial lacewings and ladybirds.

HARVESTING – WHAT'S IN SEASON?

This time of year was traditionally known as "The Hungry Gap" (cue scary mood music) because of the dearth of fresh vegetables. The efficient GIYer thumbs their nose at the notion of a hungry gap and this month is enjoying (from the ground and from storage) onions, leeks, parsnips, potatoes, sprouting broccoli, kale, rhubarb, chard, the first of the spring cauliflowers and cabbage, and spinach (perpetual). Under cover in the polytunnel or greenhouse you could also be harvesting lettuce and oriental greens such as mizuna, pak choi, mustard, oriental rocket etc.

Veg of the Month - *Cabbage*

WHY GROW IT?

Pair it with bacon or shred it for a slaw, cabbage is a supremely useful, healthy vegetable that grows well in our relatively cool climate and is relatively easy to grow. With a little planning it's also possible to have a supply of cabbage all year round, even through the coldest of winters. If it has a downside, it's that it's very vulnerable to pests.

SOWING

A foolproof way to grow healthy cabbage seedlings is to sow them in module seed trays – sow one or two seeds in each module 1.5cm deep. Thin out the weaker seedling. Cabbages will germinate in about a week and will be ready for planting about a month later. Make sure to harden off early sowings carefully. A suggested planting plan for a near continuous supply of cabbage (assuming you have the space):

- **Summer Cabbage** – sow early April
- **Autumn Cabbage** – sow early May
- **Winter Cabbage** – sow early June
- **Spring Cabbage** – sow early August

GROWING

The key with cabbage is to plant in to firm ground – think about it this way: the root and stem will eventually have to support a very heavy head! Since they are a hungry crop, add plenty of compost or manure the previous autumn. Water plants well before sowing – create a hole with a dibber, pop the seedling in and then firm in very well. Spacing will determine the size of the heads - between 45-60cm is about right. Cabbages will tolerate partial shade. Include cabbages in your brassica rotation – do not plant them where there have been brassicas for at least 3-4 years previously. Hoe around young seedlings regularly to keep weeds down. Water regularly to prevent the roots from drying out. Earthing up stems will help the plant to support the head, particularly in a windy site.

HARVESTING

Harvest spring and summer cabbages as soon as they have formed good compact heads. Autumn and winter cabbages will stand much longer in the ground, but you can lift them and store in a cool shed if you want to clear your beds for the winter. Harvest by cutting through the base of the stem.

GIY RECOMMENDED VARIETIES

Vertus (Savoy), Hispi (Spring), Stonehead (Summer), Marner Lagerfeld, January King (Winter).

PROBLEMS

Cabbage root fly maggots eat the roots causing the plant to stop growing. Prevention is better than cure – 15cm wide "collars" made from felt or carpet placed around the stem at soil level, can prevent the adult fly from laying its eggs. The other major pests are butterfly (large and small white) and moths which lay their eggs on the underside of leaves – the resulting caterpillars will munch their way through your crop in no time. You can remove the caterpillars as they appear, but again the best option is prevention – cover your cabbage crop with appropriate netting to stop the butterfly laying its eggs on the leaves. A more serious (though less prevelent) problem is clubroot, a fungus which can stay in the soil for up to 20 years.

GIY TIPS

- You can test to see if the young seedling is planted firmly enough as follows: after planting, tug at a leaf – the leaf should pull off (as opposed to pulling the whole seedling out of the ground).
- After harvesting a cabbage head, cut a cross in to the stem – if left in the soil, each quadrant in the stem will sprout baby cabbage leaves which effectively gives you a second crop from the one plant.

MONTHLY INSIGHT – SOWING SEEDS

TOP 3 TIPS ON SEEDS

- Always buy good quality seed, organic if possible.
- Seeds are perishable - store them carefully, if possible in a sealed tin somewhere cool and dry.
- Keep an eye on the "sow before" dates on your seed packets – old seed generally will not germinate as successfully as new seed.

SEEDS CAN BE SOWN:

- Direct in to the soil.
- In a pot, tray or module tray (a tray with individual compartments in it) and transplanted later.

In my opinion (and though it's creating additional work), you are better off to sow seeds in pots or trays and then transplant them out in to the soil later. This is because plants are at their most vulnerable (to poor weather and pests such as slugs) in their first 3-6 weeks. Sowing seeds in pots/trays allows you to get the seedlings to the stage where they are good and hardy before planting out. You can also get a head start on the growing season, keeping the pots/trays indoors during early spring when it is generally too cold to sow outside. I sow the following seeds direct in the soil: carrots, parsnips, broad beans, dwarf French beans, peas, potatoes, onions and shallots (sets), and garlic. Pretty much everything else I sow in module trays for later planting.

POTTING COMPOST

Potting compost used for seed sowing (not to be confused with the compost made from kitchen or garden waste) is a sterile medium which means you know there are no weed seeds in it. It also retains moisture very effectively which is important for your seeds. Interestingly, potting compost is low in nutrients so it is only ever used for starting seeds off – if you intend to grow a plant to maturity in a pot, it will need to be transplanted in to a medium that has more nutrients in it (e.g. a mix of compost and soil).

Keep the potting compost moist – this is crucial, particularly when you are waiting on seeds to germinate. If you are providing heat to seed trays in early spring, it can be challenging to prevent the potting compost from drying out. I often cover pots/trays with cling film or plastic covers (recycled plastic fruit punnets work well for this) which retains moisture and reduces the need for watering. Remove the covering as soon as the seeds germinate. When watering small seeds use a fine rose head on your watering can – the water comes out in a fine mist.

SOWING SEEDS – THE PROCESS

1 Put compost in to the container (tray or pot), overfilling. Give the container a few bangs on the table to help the compost to settle down and remove air pockets. Over-fill again and then use a ruler or a flat piece of timber to "cut" the excess off, leaving a level surface.

2 Water the compost well and let it drain.

3 Sow the seed to the depth specified on the seed packet – the bigger the seed the deeper it goes. Tiny celery or lettuce seeds simply sit on top of the compost and aren't covered. A larger pumpkin seed for example is pushed down in to the compost and covered over.

4 Label with details of veg type, date sown and variety. I use plastic plant labels, and a pencil so they are reusable.

5 Keep the compost moist throughout its time in the container.

Above: The heated bench in the potting shed.

MARCH TIPS

SEED PACKET EDUCATION

- Always read the back of seed packets – more often than not, the information on the back of a seed packet will tell you the vast majority of information you need to know about growing that particular vegetable!

HOW TO DEAL WITH LEGGY SEEDLINGS

A common problem with seedlings (particularly early spring sowings) is that they become "leggy" - this happens because there's not enough light available and the seedlings are essentially reaching to get to whatever light is available. The "legginess" will be accompanied by them veering in the direction of whatever light is available. Simply running your hand gently over and back through the seedlings will help. Do it each day, up to twenty times at a go, and it encourages a bit of hardiness in the seedlings - much as a light breeze would do.

UPCYCLE

Your recycle bin can often throw up very useful veggie-growing aids in the shape of pots, containers, cloches and seed sowing containers.

- Yogurt pots are great for starting tomato, pepper, and aubergine seeds - poke a few drainage holes in the bottom and they are perfect for the purpose.
- Egg cartons are great for chitting spuds in, but they are also good for seed sowing so long as you are not sowing seeds in them that need a large root system.
- Toilet roll inserts are brilliant to sow in - pretty much anything can be sown in them and they can be placed directly in to the soil as the insert will then rot away - this minimises the amount of disturbing that happens to the root (very important for successful transplanting).
- Use clear plastic punnets, pots and containers – don't toss em! They can act as cloches in that crucial springtime period when seedlings are first put out in the soil.
- Cut the bottom off a large 2l milk carton. Then bury the carton, spout-down, in the ground beside a tomato or cucumber plant and water in to it. This makes watering easier and gets 2l of water direct to the roots of these deep-rooting plants.

5 TIPS FOR LOOKING AFTER YOUR SOIL

- Love your soil. Healthy soil = healthy you.
- Don't walk on beds ever, especially when wet.
- Be wary of overdigging and avoid rotavating - it destroys soil structure.
- Apply bulky manures or compost annually – a 5 to 7cm covering on all your beds.
- Keep soil covered, particularly in winter - bare soil is unnatural in nature. Mulch, sow green manures or cover with black polythene or cardboard.

Buttered Cabbage

Irish people usually boil cabbage for ages, so when I cooked it this way on my TV programme some years ago it caused a sensation. This method takes only a few minutes to cook but first the cabbage must be carefully sliced into fine shreds. It should be served the moment it is cooked.

SERVES 4

450g (1lb) fresh Savoy cabbage

25-50g (1-2oz) butter

salt and freshly ground pepper

a knob of butter

From Darina Allen's Ballymaloe Cookery Course by Darina Allen. Kyle Cathie 2000.

Remove the tough outer leaves from the cabbage. Cut into quarters, remove the core, then slice into fine shreds across the grain. Put 2-3 tablespoons of water into a wide saucepan with the butter and a pinch of salt. Bring to the boil, add the cabbage and toss constantly over a high heat, then cover for a few minutes. Take care it doesn't boil dry. Toss again and add some more salt, freshly ground pepper and a knob of butter. Serve immediately.

Chinese Seaweed (Deep-fried Cabbage)

Surprisingly, the 'crispy dried seaweed' served in many Chinese restaurants is no such thing – merely deep-fried cabbage shreds. This original way of cooking cabbage tastes absolutely delicious and once you start to eat it, just like peanuts or popcorn, it is quite addictive.

Savoy cabbage or spring green cabbage

salt

sugar

From Darina Allen's Ballymaloe Cookery Course by Darina Allen. Kyle Cathie 2000.

Remove the stalks from the outer leaves.

Roll the dry leaves into a cigar shape and slice with a very sharp knife into the finest possible shreds.

Heat the oil in a deep-fryer to 180°C/350°F.

Toss in some of the cabbage and cook for a few seconds. As soon as it starts to crisp, remove and drain on kitchen paper.

Sprinkle with salt and sugar, toss and serve cold.

Bean and Kale Soup

DORCAS BARRY

SERVES 4

1 tbsp olive oil

1 onion, chopped finely

2 carrots, peeled and chopped into cubes

2 sticks of celery, washed and chopped into cubes

2 cloves garlic, peeled and sliced

1 ½ tsp pimentón (smoked paprika)

1 tsp harissa (I like Belazu Rose Harissa best)

1 x 400g tin cannellini beans, rinsed

1 stalk Kombu (optional)

750ml vegetable stock

6-8 stalks of curly kale

salt & pepper

sprouted seeds to serve (optional)

From Dorcas Barry www.dorcasbarry.com

Heat the oil in a saucepan and add the chopped onion, carrots and celery. Allow to sauté gently over a medium heat for 10-15 minutes until softened. Add the sliced garlic and stir, allowing to cook for a moment before adding the beans, the harissa, and the smoked paprika. Keep stiring to combine the spices.

Pour in the vegetable stock and allow the soup to cook for at least 30 minutes, giving the flavours time to combine and the beans to cook. It's a great idea when cooking with beans to include a stalk of dried kombu seaweed (available from delis and healthfood shops) which helps to soften the beans but also boosts the mineral content of any dish. If you include it, remove from the soup before serving.

Wash the kale well and cut out the stalks. Chop both the stalks and the leaves and add the stalks to the soup as they will take longer to cook. Add the chopped kale leaves to the soup 5 minutes before serving to ensure the kale leaves are not overcooked and are bright green in colour. Taste the soup and adjust the seasoning as required.

Ladle into bowls and served sprinkled with mixed sprouted seeds.

MAKES 2-3 JARS

60g flour

15g ginger powder

80g mustard powder

25g turmeric powder

500ml vinegar

130g sugar

100ml ginger syrup

300g cauliflower rosettes (small)

2 onions, diced in cubes

100g cucumber, diced in cubes

50g carrot, diced in cubes

pepper and salt

From *Cliff House Hotel – The Cookbook*, Written by Martijn Kajuiter & edited by Tom Doorley. Published by Houghton Mifflin Harcourt Trade 2009.

Piccalilli

MARTIJN KAJUITER

Sweat the onions in a saucepan with a little oil. Add the flour, ginger, mustard and turmeric. Heat through for 60 seconds and set aside.

Bring the vinegar to the boil and add the cauliflower rosettes, carrots and cucumber. Cook until the cauliflower is tender, then strain. Put the vegetables aside.

Add the ginger syrup and sugar to the vinegar. Pour onto the flour and spice mix and whisk to remove any lumps. Simmer this mixture for 10 minutes.

Add the vegetables and bring to the boil. Simmer for a further 10 minutes. Season to taste. Put into a clean jar and keep in the fridge.

Purple Sprouting Broccoli and Hollandaise

TOM DOORLEY & JOHANN DOORLEY

The flavour of purple sprouting broccoli (PSB) is like refined cabbage, but not cabbagey. We put it on a par with asparagus as a seasonal treat. It's mainly only available to home gardeners, as it rarely makes it to the supermarkets. Country markets and farmers' markets do get it, but the season is short. We share the first small picks of PSB as a starter with melted butter or some hollandaise. As it gets more abundant, we use it in quiche or as a vegetable with a main course. We find steaming is the best method of cooking PSB, as it doesn't make it overly wet and it's easier to test for doneness.

purple sprouting broccoli,
4-6 stalks per person

TOM'S HOLLANDAISE

50g (2oz) salted butter

100g (4oz) unsalted butter

1 shallot

2 tbsp water

1 tbsp white wine vinegar

1 large egg yolk

From *Grow & Cook* by Tom Doorley and Johann Doorley. Published by Gill & Macmillan Ltd 2007.

To prepare the PSB, trim into even lengths and place in a steamer basket. Bring 5cm (2 inches) of water to the boil in the bottom of the steamer. Put the steamer basket on top with the lid on and steam for 3-5 minutes. Test with a fork that the stems are tender and remove from the steamer when done. Pat the PSB with kitchen paper to remove excess moisture. Divide the PSB onto warm plates and spoon over a little melted butter or hollandaise sauce.

To make the hollandaise sauce, cut the butter into 2 cm (¾ inch) cubes and allow them to warm up to room temperature. Peel and slice the shallot. Pour the water and vinegar into a small saucepan and add the shallot. Put the pot on to the boil. Boil the liquid until it's reduced to only one dessertspoonful. Remove from the heat and strain the reduced liquid into the top of a double boiler and discard the shallot.

Put 5 cm (2 inches) of very hot water into the bottom of the double boiler and place on a very low heat. The water in the bottom of the double boiler should be hot, but not boiling, so that the steam heats the top. Add the egg yolk to the vinegar and whisk them together for a moment before putting the top onto the double boiler. Whisk until the egg starts to thicken, then add the butter a cube at a time, until all the butter is added and the sauce is thick.

If it gets too hot and starts to crack, take the top off the double boiler and whisk in 4 or 5 cubes of butter in one go to cool it down. If you want to be extra safe, have a bowl of really cold water in the sink that you can cool the top of the double boiler.

Using 4 to 6 stalks of purple sprouting broccoli per person, trim the PSB, place in a steamer basket and steam over boiling water for about 3-4 minutes. The stems should give to a fork and the tops should be bright green. Place on kitchen paper to dry for a moment and then onto hot plates. Pour over some hollandaise sauce and serve.

April

ISN'T IT JUST THE MOST WONDERFUL time of the year? All of nature is in major growth mode – the most detested weed and the most beloved seedlings are growing almost in front of our eyes. Leaves are emerging on trees and flowers appearing in the garden practically overnight. I am spending night and day in the veggie patch at the moment (particularly on weekends) and if I was asked I couldn't tell you whether it's because there's so much work to do, or because I love it so much.

There is a lot to do in April. Sowing loads of seeds, getting ground prepared in the veg patch for outdoor sowing, watering the tunnel, keeping on top of weeds, hardening off seedlings (which means ferrying them in and out morning and evening). I find the best way for me to stay on top of all the work is to sneak in some time in the garden every day, rather than leaving it all until the weekend. I'm an early riser anyway, so I'll happily spend twenty minutes in the veg patch in the morning before work. And of course with the long evenings I just feel guilty about sitting down to watch TV when I could be out forking over a bed to get it ready for seedlings. Still, being out in the vegetable patch is calming for the soul – it's an incredibly meditative and stress-busting pastime.

THIS MONTH'S TOP JOBS

* Monthly indoor sowing of lettuce, oriental greens, annual spinach, calabrese, coriander.

* Sow indoors: summer cabbage, kohlrabi, brussels sprouts, beetroot (2), celery (2), courgette, kale, perpetual spinach, swede, chard.

* Sow outdoors: peas, onion sets, shallots and main crop potatoes.

* Harden off seedlings about a week before they are due to be planted outside.

Left: *The potting shed – the seedy side of town.*

Things to Do in... April

PREPARATION

April is the banker month - if poor weather in March has hampered your outdoor work, then April is the month to catch up. Fork over and rake the soil in preparation for the crops.

TO DO LIST

Two words; weeds and slugs. You need to stay on top of them both. 'Earth-up' your spuds - this means drawing up soil around the stems which creates additional depth of soil and therefore encourages the plants to produce more potatoes. A ridging hoe is the ideal tool for earthing up. Water your tunnel/greenhouse – things can get pretty warm on a nice sunny April day and seedlings will dry out quickly. As the weather improves, ventilate the polytunnel during the day. Cabbage root fly attack brassicas by laying eggs at the base of plants. Cut discs of soft material, like carpet underlay and lay flat around the base of the plant. Depending on the weather, cabbage butterflies will also soon be laying eggs. Check the undersides of leaves and scrape off eggs before they hatch. You will need to keep this vigilance up in the coming months - collect the caterpillars and feed to the hens.

SOWING SEEDS

Sow indoors: oriental greens, lettuce, annual spinach, summer cabbage, kohlrabi, Brussels sprouts, beetroot, celery, courgette, kale, perpetual spinach, swede and chard. Sow direct in the soil outdoors: peas, onion sets, shallots and main crop potatoes.

PLANTING OUT

Hardening off – seeds raised indoors/under cover, need to be acclimatised outdoors before planting out. Bring them outside during daylight hours for at least a week. Plant out cabbage plants when they are 15/20 cm tall into well prepared soil that has been manured. Water the plants well the day before and lift each plant with as big a root ball as possible. Firm the plants in well and water. Tomato plants might be ready for planting out in to the greenhouse/polytunnel ground this month but hold off if the weather is very cold. If space is at a premium, use plant pots to grow herbs and strawberries.

Top left: *Polytunnel with recently planted tomatoes.*

Bottom left: *A message to slugs, written in hope rather than expectation.*

HARVESTING – WHAT'S IN SEASON?

Stored fruit and vegetables are likely to be a distant memory at this stage and new crops are only starting to trickle in which makes April a tricky proposition. The middle of this month might see the first asparagus and the first early spring cabbage. The other two star performers this month are sprouting broccoli and rhubarb. You could also be harvesting leeks, spring cauliflowers, kale, spinach and chard, lettuce, carrots (in polytunnel), radish, spring onions and wild garlic. Pick bundles of tender young nettles - divert some to the kitchen for a delicious nettle soup or blood-purifying tea and use the rest for an organic fertilizer. Nettles are extremely high in nitrogen so if you soak a large bucketful in water for a week, you produce a brilliant nitrogen-rich fertilizer which will be hugely beneficial for any plants which need leafy growth, for example lettuces, cabbage, kale etc. Put a kilo of nettles in a hessian bag and soak in 20 litres of water and leave it to stew for a month or so. It gets pretty stink so put a lid on top. Mix one part nettle liquid with ten parts water when applying to plants.

Veg of the Month - *Lettuce*

WHY GROW IT?

Because it's so perishable, it's always difficult to find good quality, fresh lettuce in the supermarkets. Lettuce is easy to grow and with a little planning, you can eat it fresh for 9 months of the year.

SOWING

There are four main types of lettuce. The first three - butterheads, cos and crispheads - form hearts at their centre and are therefore usually grown as proper heads of lettuce. They take longer to mature. The fourth type - loose-leaf - doesn't form a heart and is therefore generally grown as a "cut-and-come-again" crop – where leaves are cut as required. I rarely let any of my lettuce plants form a 'head', taking individual leaves off instead (outer leaves first) and allowing the plant to grow back so I can get a second and even third flush of leaves from the same plant.

I always sow lettuce seeds in module trays, making a shallow indentation in the compost in each module with my finger and popping a single seed in to it. Lettuce needs light to germinate so don't cover the seeds with compost. Lettuce will not germinate in temperatures above 25 degrees celsius so if the weather is very warm you may need to move the trays in to a cool shed for a few days until they germinate. Seedlings are ready to plant out when they have 4 or 5 leaves. Harden off well before transplanting. I generally plant lettuce out in to my polytunnel except in the summer months.

GROWING

Lettuce will do well in any reasonable soil, as long as it's moisture retentive – add well-rotted manure or compost the previous winter. Lettuce is a great space filler – you can pop it anywhere you have some space, and it doesn't need to fit in with your crop rotation plans. Spacing is about 20-30cm depending on the type. Plant the seedlings well down in the soil with the cotyledons (seed leaves) just above the soil level. Keep the soil around the plants weed free and water copiously in dry weather – this will help prevent them bolting.

HARVESTING

You can leave cos, butterhead and crisphead varieties of lettuce longer to develop their hearts. Cut leaves of loose-leaf varieties as soon as they are of usable size. If you cut them about 5cm from the ground they will grow back and you will be able to take a second crop in a few weeks. Harvest lettuce leaves early in the day and they will keep far longer. This is because later in the day the moisture has evaporated from the leaves and so it wilts more quickly.

GIY RECOMMENDED VARIETIES

Mixed Leaf, Dynamite, Little Gem, Brandon, Iceberg, Aruba.

PROBLEMS

Slugs eat young leaves and get in to the hearts of lettuces. Aphids (black or greenfly) can be a problem. Leatherjackets (the larvae of the Daddy Longlegs) eat through the stems of newly planted lettuce. Lack of water causes the plants to panic and run to seed in a desperate attempt to reproduce before they die! This is called "bolting" and it's very bad news as the plants are too bitter to eat.

GIY TIPS

- Sow successionally – I sow one or two 8-module trays at the start of every month for a continuous supply.
- Try growing summer lettuce in partial shade – they don't like hot weather.

MONTHLY INSIGHT– GROWING HERBS

Herbs have a multitude of uses in the home and garden, but mainly we grow them because they taste amazing! Even if you don't grow a lot of your own food, you can make any meal feel homegrown by adding some of your own herbs. Also, bear in mind that shop-bought herbs are expensive and usually imported. You will save a lot of money by having a good crop of herbs at hand, since you can simply snip off as much as you need for a particular dish, which reduces waste. So, get growing and say goodbye to those plastic containers of herbs that tend to go off down the back of your fridge!

Most herbs are easy to grow, and can be grown in containers – so even if you don't have much space you can get involved. Herbs are divided into two main groups - those which you have to sow annually from seed such as basil and coriander, and those which are a more permanent feature in the garden such as mint and rosemary. Given how long they will last, I think it's a good investment to buy healthy plants of the latter. Herbs can be grown in the open ground or in containers (pots, troughs, bags or whatever is available). It is best to use a soil based growing medium (as opposed to potting compost), fed with plenty of homemade compost. Most herbs require a sunny location to thrive. Over the following pages you can read about the most common herbs, how to grow them and their traditional uses.

GEMMA HUGHES

ANNUAL HERBS

BASIL — Part used: leaf. Aids stomach spasms and bloating. Anti-inflammatory and anti-bacterial. Herbalists could never agree about basil. It was known as a love token, which would secure the love of whom it was given to. Though it was also known as "love washed with tears" in parts of Italy and Crete. The ultimate summer herb is usually sown in March/April in pots indoors and moved outdoors when the risk of frost has passed. Allow to get established before cutting (usually about 6–8 weeks after planting).

....

PARSLEY — Part used: leaf. Aids digestion, rheumatism and benefits the kidneys when it is drunk as tea. Leaves are used externally for sore eyes, insect bites and headlice. Traditionally used in the west of Ireland, under beds to rid them of fleas. A supremely useful herb for stocks, soups and stuffings, parsley can be sown in pots or in the open ground. It is very slow to germinate but hardy once you get it going.

DILL — Parts used: leaf, seed and root. A mild infusion of the seeds calms babies and helps reduce wind. When taken daily, the root and leaves are said to increase milk flow of nursing mother. Dill water was used to sweeten bad breath and leaves, eaten daily, strengthen nails and hair. In some European countries, as a good omen, brides put a sprig of dill and some salt in their shoes, as well as wearing a sprig on their gown. Can be sown in the ground in March/April. The leaves are ready for picking just before the flowers open.

....

CORIANDER — Parts used: seeds and leaf. Eases indigestion and flatulence. Sweetened with honey was a cure for worms. Valued as a love potion and aphrodisiac, old European herbal tradition used this herb to attract love. A delicious and distinctive herb, but unfortunately inclined to bolt. Sow little and often — will work in pots or in the soil. Both leaves and seeds are edible.

....

MARJORAM — Part used: leaf. It aids digestion, sweetens the breath, is a calming tonic and helps eliminate toxins from the body. Used for seasickness. Dried leaves were used as snuff to clear a blocked nose. First raised by Venus, marjoram in Roman tradition was worn as wreaths crowning the bride and groom at weddings. Can be sown indoors or outdoors in small pots or direct into the ground. The leaves are usually picked at flowering time.

BASIL

PARSLEY

DILL

MARJORAM

CORIANDER

PERENNIAL HERBS

ROSEMARY — Part used: leaf. Antiseptic. Calms nerves, headaches and tremors. Sweetens breath. Stimulates circulation and may help regulate low blood pressure. Traditionally, sprigs of rosemary were used in laundry baskets to deter moths and was worn on a roasted boars head as a garland. A sprig under the pillow was said to prevent nightmares. A cinch to grow and once you get a decent plant established it will reward you with fresh herbs for years. The bushes can grow up to 1.5m in height.

THYME — Part used: leaf. Eases indigestion, flatulence, coughs, chest colds, sore throats and stuffy noses. Bathing in thyme stimulates circulation and aids the skin. It encourages hair growth when rubbed into the scalp. Traditionally, in many countries, thyme was used to keep away fleas by burning it or laying sprigs of it between your clothes. Where would stuffing be without thyme? The seed is usually sown in April in pots or in the open ground where plants are thinned out to 15 cm apart. Golden leaved and variegated kinds are available with whole stems picked before or at flowering time.

MINT — Part used: leaf. Aids digestion, eases upset stomachs, hiccups and nausea. Traditionally leaves were used on bee and wasp stings. Plants were grown near crops to keep rodents at bay, as they do not like the strong aroma. Mint is very fast growing (some would say invasive) and ideally should be grown in pots or in pots plunged in the open ground. Seed germination is slow from outdoor sown seed.

SAGE — Part used: leaf. A tonic and a blood cleanser. Breath freshener. Aids bleeding gums and reduces excess saliva. Used to protect against a sore throat. Also, for rheumatism relief and nervous headaches. An old saying from medieval times is; "Why should a man die when sage grows in his garden?". *Salvia*, the Latin for sage, means 'to save'. Sage is a bushy plant with woody stems, green grey leaves and purple flowers. It is easily grown from seed and the leaves are usually picked before or at flowering time. The flowers are beautiful which is a bonus.

TARRAGON — Part used: leaf. Aids digestion by stimulation. May prevent colic, wind and flatulence. Part of the Latin name, *dracunculus*, is so called because the roots curl back on themselves like a dragons tail. The root traditionally was used to aid toothache, muscle pain, dog and dragon bites! The herb is sown in pots in April under protection and then planted on. It is best managed when transplanted into a container and overwintered indoors. The plant can grow up to 1 metre tall.

ROSEMARY

THYME

SAGE

MINT

TARRAGON

APRIL TIPS

KOHLRABI

Kohlrabi is gaining in popularity and little wonder – it's quick-growing, relatively easy to grow and tastes great, cooked or raw. Available as green, white or purple varieties, kohlrabi stems grow above the ground. Do a sowing in April under cover indoors for later transplanting outside. Here are some things you may not know about kohlrabi:

- Raw kohlrabi is delicious in coleslaws.
- It's a brassica so include it in your crop rotation.
- The green varieties mature quicker.
- Kohlrabi do not store well so harvest as required.

PLAN A LETTUCE SUPPLY

Nothing beats the flavour, freshness or variety of your own home-grown lettuce - it's also pretty easy to grow. It makes sense therefore to put some thought in to guaranteeing a year-round supply and ensuring you don't have any gaps. At the start of each month from February to September, I sow one or two 8-module trays (with various varieties) for planting out about a month later. This gives me a continuous supply. In September I do a decent sowing of winter-hardy lettuce and oriental greens for an over-winter polytunnel supply. Early sowings are on a sunny windowsill or heated propagation mat.

FORAGE

Dandelion A single dandelion leaf contains your recommended daily allowance of vitamin C and is also a very good source of vitamin A. Dandelions are a forager's dream - a plant that grows abundantly (often in your back garden), that can be eaten raw in salads, is incredibly good for you, and absolutely FREE! Dandelion is relatively easy to identify - it has bright yellow flowers and green jagged leaves. Leaves are best picked when young as they can get bitter later in life and they are excellent raw in salads. You can add them to soup and also cook them like spinach (soak in salt water for 30 mins first). And you thought it was a weed?!

Sorrel can be grown, but it can also be foraged and from now until late October, it can be found growing wild. There are two main types – sheep sorrel which has broad leaves and wood sorrel which has three leaves. Sheep sorrel looks a lot like spinach and is to be found in gardens, ditches and fields – at the base of the leaf it has a highly distinctive arrow shape. Wood sorrel is found in woodlands. Both have a slightly sour, lemony flavour and can be used in salads, soups, stews and sauces. It can also be preserved in oil.

Right: *Kohlrabi – almost too good-looking to pick.*

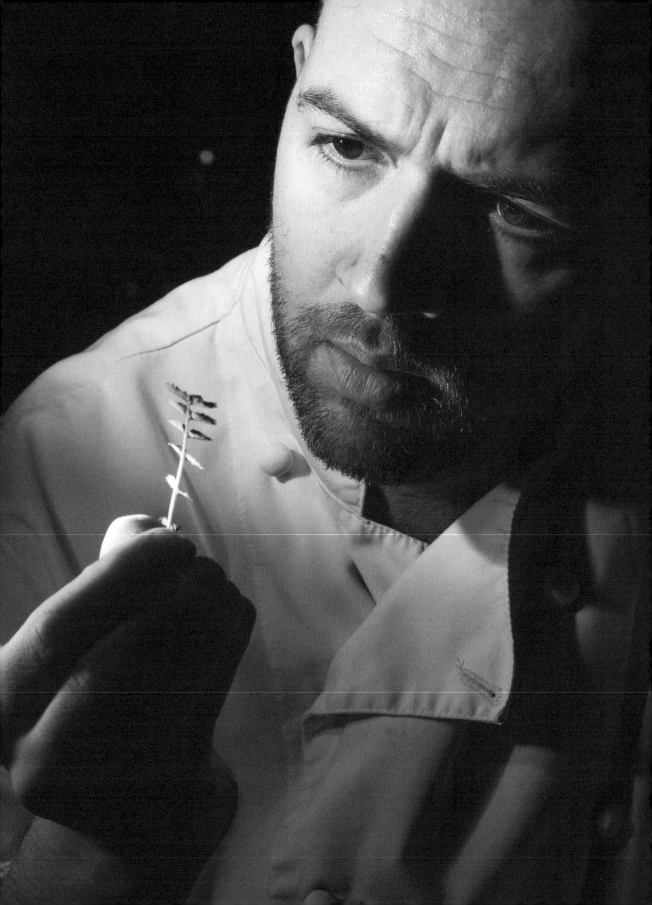

Orange Salad

SERVES 2-4

ORANGE DRESSING

500ml fresh orange juice

zest of two oranges

30g castor sugar

100ml water

400ml sunflower oil

25g coriander seeds, roasted and crushed

FOR THE SALAD

washed rocket and mixed lettuce leaves

1 cucumber (peeled, deseeded and finely sliced)

2 oranges, segmented

half of a lemon

50g candied walnuts (make a caramel of 100g sugar and 50g water, then add peeled walnut and stir to separate)

picked coriander

picked tarragon

PICKLED CARROT STRINGS

2 peeled carrots (peeled carrots sliced length ways on mandolin and julienned)

300ml water

100g sugar

100ml white wine vinegar

sprig of thyme

From Dylan McGrath www.dylanmcgrath.com

To make the orange dressing

Place the orange juice, zest and sugar into a heavy bottom pan and reduce until sticky. Skim off any impurity that comes to the surface.

While the reduction is still warm put it in a jug blender on full speed and slowly add the vinegar, water and oil to make an emulsion.

Add the zest and juice from two oranges.

Fold in the warm crushed coriander seeds. Let rest for at least a day before you use it and do not refrigerate.

To make the pickled carrot strings

Add all ingredients into a small saucepan, bring to the boil and pour over carrot strings. Leave to cool.

To serve

In a large salad bowl, add all the salad ingredients. Season with salt. Add the coriander, tarragon, pickled carrot strings and walnuts. Add the orange dressing to coat the leaves and a squeeze of lemon juice.

Cauliflower Pakoras with Raita

MARK DIACONO

I would eat these pakoras every day, they are so good. The batter works equally well coating Romanesco, calabrese, sliced onions and most root veg. I usually eat them with the minty, poppy seed raita, below.

SERVES 3-4

1 medium cauliflower

3 onions

140g chickpea flour

1 tsp bicarbonate of soda

1 tsp ground cumin

1 tsp ground turmeric

1 tsp ground ginger

1 tsp garam masala

1 tsp salt

about 100ml water

sunflower oil for deep-frying

FOR THE RAITA

300ml natural yoghurt

a handful of mint leaves, finely shredded

2 tsp poppy seeds

TO SERVE

sea salt and freshly ground black pepper

a good sprinkling of coriander microleaves, or a half-handful of coriander, finely chopped

For the raita, combine the yoghurt, mint and poppy seeds in a bowl.

Remove and discard the outer leaves and stalk from the cauliflower, then cut it into 1cm pieces. Finely slice the onions.

To make the batter, sift the flour, bicarbonate of soda, ground spices and salt together into a large bowl. Add most of the water and mix into the flour with your fingertips, adding more of the water a little at a time, if needed, to form a thickish batter (think pricey emulsion).

Heat the oil for deep-frying in a suitable large, deep, heavy pan (it should fill no more than one-third of the pan) to about 170°C. To test the temperature, drop a small cube of bread into the oil – it should fizz and brown in about a minute.

Toss the onions and cauliflower together in a bowl. Add the batter and turn the vegetables to coat well.

You will need to cook the pakoras in batches to ensure you don't crowd the pan; I usually cook three at a time. Carefully ease a spoonful of the mixture into the hot oil. When it begins to cook, add a couple more. Turn the pakoras occasionally so that they cook and colour evenly. This should take 7-10 minutes. When they are golden brown and cooked through, lift them out with a slotted spoon onto kitchen paper to drain. Keep hot while you cook the rest.

Sprinkle the pakoras with a little sea salt, pepper and coriander, and serve with the minty raita.

From *A Year at Otter Farm* by Mark Diacono. Published by Bloomsbury, 2014.

Risotto with Spinach & Parmesan

DERRY CLARKE

SERVES 2

50g butter

1 small onion (diced finely)

300g arborio rice

1 litre chicken stock

salt and freshly ground white pepper

2 large handfuls of spinach

75g Parmesan

From Derry Clarke, *L'Ecrivain Restaurant,* Dublin.

Melt the butter in a medium sized saucepan and gently cook the onion for 5 minutes until tender.

Add the rice and stir, then cook for another 3 minutes.

Meanwhile, heat the stock in a separate saucepan.

Add the stock to the rice, ladle by ladle, stirring constantly.

Add the Parmesan and spinach when the rice is nearly fully cooked.

Continue to cook until all the stock is absorbed (about 12-14 minutes) and the rice is cooked.

Season to taste.

Rhubarb Tart

Rhubarb and spring arrive together. I love rhubarb. It's the first to wave the 'I have survived the winter' flag in my otherwise desolate garden. Last autumn I put my rhubarb to bed under a duvet of well-rotted manure. My efforts were rewarded as my rhubarb peeked above ground a month early from its winter slumber, pink and ready to be plucked.

SERVES 6-8

225g cold butter cut in small cubes

50g castor sugar

2 small eggs beaten with a dessert spoon of cold water

400g plain flour

a dessert spoon of cold water

400g fresh rhubarb, washed and chopped into 3cm pieces

150g castor sugar

finely grated zest of one orange

From Eunice Power, www.eunicepower.com

I use the traditional enamel plates to make this tart. They are about 20cm / 8 inches wide. A 20cm / 8 inch loose bottomed tart tin will work also.

To make the pastry: in a food processor blitz the flour, sugar and butter until it resembles breadcrumbs; add the eggs and water to make a non-sticky doughy consistency.

Knead the pastry on a floured surface into a ball, wrap in cling film and chill in the fridge for about 20 minutes.

After chilling, roll out ½ the pastry on a floured surface until even and wide enough to cover the tart plate.

Grease the tart plate or tin and place the pastry on top (if pastry hangs over the side don't cut it off).

Next toss the rhubarb in the sugar and orange rind, and put on the pastry base.

Roll out the remainder of the pastry and place on top of the Rhubarb. Use water to seal the pastry base and top together, and for a better seal and look, go around the edges and press down with a fork. With a sharp knife trim off the edges and pastry bits sticking out and keep for decoration.

Make a few cuts with a sharp knife on the surface of the pastry a few times to allow hot rising air to escape while cooking and decorate your Rhubarb tart in any way you please!

Wash some egg on the surface to create a glossy look when cooked and also sprinkle some sugar on top for taste and effect.

Place Rhubarb tart into a pre heated over at 180°C/350°F for 45 minutes to 1 hour.

Let the tart cool and serve on its own or with fresh cream or custard. Springtime Bliss!

Rhubarb Compote

This compote recipe is so versatile. Delicious served with granola, thick Greek yoghurt or as an addition to Champagne or Prosecco as a pretty and gratifying spring cocktail – rhubarb Bellini (see opposite page).

400g new season rhubarb, cut into 3cm pieces

finely grated rind and juice of one orange

150ml water

400g sugar

1 dessertspoon of arrowroot

Wash and slice the Rhubarb. On a gentle heat dissolve the sugar in the orange juice and water.

Allow to simmer and add the rhubarb and orange rind. Simmer for 3 to 4 minutes and turn off the heat. Allow to cool. Strain off the rhubarb and return the syrup to the saucepan. Dissolve the arrowroot in a tablespoon of water then add to the syrup. Return the syrup to the stove and simmer for 5 minutes until the syrup thickens. Take off the heat, allow to cool, return the rhubarb. And there you have wonderful compote with so many possibilities.

From Eunice Power, www.eunicepower.com

Rhubarb Granola

Granola is crunchy, nutty, sweet and spicy and was once described as 'a third layer of clothing on a cold morning'. We have this for breakfast with Greek yoghurt or loaded onto a big bowl of creamy porridge with lots of delicious compote made from rhubarb in the garden.

250g jumbo oats

100g flaked almonds

100g sunflower seeds

100g pumpkin seeds

1 teaspoon grated nutmeg

1 dessertspoon of ground cinnamon

a pinch of salt

70ml sunflower oil

70g honey

150g ready to eat apricots, cut into chunks

Pre heat the oven to 150°C. Toss the dry ingredients together except the apricots, then add the oil and the honey and mix to coat thoroughly.

Spread the mixture on two baking sheets lined with parchment paper and bake until golden, turning every 10 minutes so that it browns evenly. The granola should be ready after 30 minutes- cooking time may vary from oven to oven so keep an eye on it so that it doesn't burn.

When it comes out of the oven allow to cool and then add the apricots. As the granola cools it will lose it stickiness and become crunchy. Store in a tightly sealed jar or bag.

See previous page for picture of rhubarb compote, rhubarb granola and rhubarb Bellini.

From Eunice Power, www.eunicepower.com

Rhubarb Bellini

Pour the chilled syrup (see rhubarb compote on opposite page) into champagne flutes, and then top up with chilled Prosecco, Cava or Champagne. Stir to mix and add a few pieces of rhubarb from the compote, then top off with more Prosecco or Champagne, pouring gradually. The mixture will bubble madly for a minute!'

From Eunice Power, www.eunicepower.com

May

THOUGH MAY IS OFFICIALLY speaking late spring, May Day, which takes place on the first day of the month is traditionally a celebration of the beginning of summer. It has been celebrated as a time of growth, renewal and fertility across Europe since pre-Christian times and is one of the two great celebrations in the Celtic year (the other one is Halloween which marks the onset of winter).

Ancient May Day customs include May Bushes, maypole and sword dancing, lighting bonfires, and comely maidens bathing in the dew of a May morning to retain their beauty. So, you get the picture – basically it's a time of the year for growth, fertility and getting your kit off.

There's plenty to celebrate. After the long lean winter in the veggie patch, things are growing at a dizzying pace. Trying to keep on top of things in the veggie patch can be challenging at this time of the year. May is one of the busiest seed sowing months, and there are lots of other things to do too - weeding and watering, plants to be hardened off and staked/ supported/netted, and (whisper it) even some gentle harvesting.

THIS MONTH'S TOP JOBS

* Monthly sowing of lettuce, oriental greens, annual spinach, calabrese, coriander.

* Sow direct outside: parsnips, carrots (last week of month), dwarf French beans, peas (2).

* Sow indoors in modules or pots: sweetcorn, cucumber, squash, pumpkin, Climbing French beans and runner beans, Florence fennel, melon, Swiss chard, leeks (2), cauliflower (2), kohlrabi (2), Brussels sprouts (2), beetroot (3), celery (3), swede (2).

* Regularly hoe weeds, mulch and earth up spuds.

* Put up supports for pea and bean plants. Cover brassicas with netting.

Things to Do in... *May*

PREPARATION

Finish preparing remaining beds for early summer sowing. May is the time to get those outdoor beds ready for early summer transplanting. Fork over and rake. Don't tread!

TO DO LIST

Earth up potatoes as the plants develop – covering the stem with soil encourages potato growth. If you sow carrots in April or May, put protective barrier (enviromesh) around your carrots to thwart the dastardly carrot root fly. Or alternatively leave it until late May/early June to sow carrots as I do, and you should avoid them altogether. Regularly hoe weeds and mulch. Hoe on a dry day if possible, so the weeds shrivel up and die after hoeing.

Water outdoors if required and also continue your watering and ventilation routine in the polytunnel or greenhouse. Support tomato plants as they grow and remove the side shoots as they appear (in the angle between the stem and the trusses). As plants start to flower, tap the flowers to spread pollen and improve fruiting. Regular watering of tomato plants prevents later fruit splitting. Be vigilant for pests and diseases (e.g. carrot root fly, aphids, caterpillars, rabbits, slugs and snails). Support your pea and bean plants outside in the veg patch – boxing your broad bean plants in with string tied around bamboo canes should be sufficient. Peas require twiggy sticks, pea netting, timber supports with chicken wire, or an existing fence or hedge. Pinch out the growing tips of broad beans plants to help prevent blackfly.

SOWING SEEDS

May is a good month for sowing, and many of the crops you sow in May will catch up with seeds sown in earlier months. In addition to your monthly salad leaf sowing, sow direct outside: parsnips, carrots (last week of month), dwarf French beans, peas (2). Sow indoors in modules or pots: sweetcorn, cucumber, squash, pumpkin, climbing French beans and runner beans, Florence fennel, melon, Swiss chard, leeks (2), cauliflower (2), kohlrabi (2), Brussels sprouts (2), beetroot (3), celery (3), swede (2). You could also try an extra harvest of early spuds by planting an additional row wherever you can accommodate them.

Right: Hardening off seedlings.

PLANTING OUT

Harden off and begin to plant out seedlings you have lovingly raised indoors – e.g. celery, celeriac, Brussels sprouts, turnips, sprouting broccoli, cabbages, sweet corn, leeks and so on. Protect them from slugs and net the brassicas to prevent cabbage white butterfly from laying their eggs on the plant leaves. Tomatoes, cucumber, peppers, chilli-pepper and aubergines are planted out in the polytunnel or greenhouse and therefore won't need hardening off.

HARVESTING – WHAT'S IN SEASON?

May is another tricky "gap" month as stores continue to dwindle. You may however start getting some new spuds, particularly if you sowed an early crop in the polytunnel back in February. Continue picking asparagus, radish, rhubarb, cabbage, cauliflower, spinach and chard. May is likely to see the first real bumper salad leaves like lettuce and rocket – as well as the first garlic, beetroot, baby carrots and globe artichokes.

Veg of the Month - *Potatoes*

WHY GROW IT?

Where would the GIYer be without the humble spud? Spuds can be grown pretty much anywhere and will actually improve poor soil, their root systems breaking up soil and making it more friable. They produce a high yield from a relatively small space and store well. No wonder they have been a staple diet for Irish families for centuries. Digging for your first new potatoes will be like Christmas morning – promise!

SOWING

Effectively there are two types of potatoes – earlies and maincrop. Earlies grow quickly, have no skin worth speaking of, and are usually out of the soil before blight arrives. Maincrop develop later, produce a higher yield, develop a thick skin and can therefore be stored – they are, unfortunately, more vulnerable to blight as they are in the ground during the summer months when blight conditions prevail. Potatoes are grown from "seed potatoes" which are potatoes saved from the previous year's crop. It was traditional for Irish GIYers to save their own seed potatoes but this is generally out of favour now – better to buy certified seed potatoes each year, in case your own potatoes carry over a virus.

"Chitting" the seed potatoes is allowing them to sprout to give them a head start before sowing. Start this process in February – lay the seed potatoes out in a shallow tray or used egg cartons and leave them somewhere relatively bright and cool. By March they will have developed green sprouts. I pick off all but a couple of the sprouts before planting.

The soil in which you are planting potatoes requires a generous application of well-rotted farmyard manure, compost or seaweed before planting (ideally the previous winter). Too much nitrogen however encourages leafy growth at the expense of the tubers. Sow first earlies in mid-March (St. Patrick's Day traditionally) in single rows, 15cm deep, 25cm apart and 45cm between rows. Maincrop spuds are sown in mid to late April. Increase spacing to 35cm. It is vitally important to include potatoes in your crop rotation as they are susceptible to disease if grown in the same ground year on year. To plant a spud I simply make a 15cm deep hole with my hand and then pop the spud in.

GROWING

Cover young plants if there is any risk of frost. Potatoes require "earthing up" – this is a process of covering the stem (also called a "haulm") with soil. Since the potatoes grow along the haulm, the more of it that is buried beneath the soil, the more spuds you get. Use a ridging hoe to bring loose soil from around the plant up against the stem, particularly when the plants are young. Earthing up becomes more difficult as the plant gets taller. Repeat once or twice during the summer, particularly if you see spuds popping through the soil – spuds go green if exposed to the light and are inedible (and poisonous).

HARVESTING

Check earlies in mid-June to see how they are getting on. Earlies will be ready about 14 weeks after sowing. Maincrops take 18 weeks. The presence of flowers on the plant is often (but not always) an indicator that the spuds are ready. We typically leave our earlies in the ground and dig as required. Their thin skins mean they

Top left: *Drying out spuds before winter storage.*

don't store well but they do fine in the ground until September at which point we move on to maincrop. Maincrop can stay in the ground until the first frosts – but they are susceptible to scab, worms and slug damage so probably best to lift and store in sacks in October/November. Be sure to remove all spuds from the ground, even the tiny ones, when harvesting – if left in the soil they will sprout next year, causing problems for the crops that are planted there.

GIY RECOMMENDED VARIETIES

Orla and Homeguard (earlies), Record, Cara, Pink Fir Apple and British Queens (maincrop), Sarpo Mira (maincrop blight resistant).

PROBLEMS

Frost damage is a real problem for early sowings. Earthing up helps. Common scab on the skin of potatoes looks bad but doesn't affect the spud. Slugs are a real problem, eating holes in to the spuds. The fungal disease potato blight is the bane of the potato grower – the first symptoms are dark decaying spots on leaves. Heavy rainfall and warm, humid conditions are ideal blight environments. Use blight resistant varieties such as Sarpo Mira, Orla, Setanta and Cara.

GIY TIPS

▪ When storing maincrop potatoes, cut the stems down and leave the spuds in the ground for 10 days to allow the skin to mature. Store potatoes in hessian sacks in a dark, cool shed – do not store any damaged ones.
▪ If blight strikes, cut down the stems immediately, leaving the tubers in the ground – they won't grow any more, but the blight won't reach them.

MONTHLY INSIGHT – GIYing IN RAISED BEDS

GIYing in raised beds is increasingly popular mainly because it overcomes the problems of poor soil quality and drainage. Raised beds are an ingenious cheat to quickly provide good quality, deep, fertile soil that's perfect for planting.

5 BENEFITS OF RAISED BED GROWING

- You can put a few raised beds on top of a lawn, fill with soil, and start growing instantly, with no back-breaking digging.
- You don't stand on the soil - less soil compaction and better drainage.
- Extra depth of soil means plants can develop good root systems.
- Gravel or bark mulch pathways around them mean that the beds can be accessed all year round.
- A raised bed is easier to maintain (weed, dig etc.) than a large area of open ground.

ASPECT, SHAPE AND SIZE

Choose a sunny, sheltered, well-drained spot for your beds. A 1.2m (4ft) wide bed which is 30cm (10-12 inches) deep is considered ideal. The length of it doesn't really matter – the important thing is that you should be able to reach in to the centre of the bed from both sides. Some of my raised beds are up to 5m long. I had triangular shaped raised beds some years ago, which looked pretty, but were very impractical and I subsequently took them out and replaced them with rectangular ones.

MATERIALS

You can buy raised beds or make them yourself from salvaged timber. If you are buying planks of wood, try to source un-treated timber. I used railway sleepers which were lying around my garden for mine – this is generally frowned upon and raises lots of "tut-tuts" as they apparently leech creosote and other chemicals in to the soil. But I thought it better to use them than not, and so I lined the insides of them and used away!

Main photo: *Raised beds with gravel paths for ease of maintenance.*

HOW TO BUILD A RAISED BED

1 Decide on your bed design and where you are going to put it. Measure out the lengths of wood needed, cut them to size and nail them together.

2 When filled with soil there will be quite a bit of pressure on the sides of the bed, so nail the planks to timber pegs for support.

3 Place a layer of wet cardboard or newspaper at the bottom to kill off grass and weeds.

4 Fill with alternating layers of manure/compost and top soil – aim for a mix of 60% soil and 40% compost/manure.

5 Start growing.

MAY TIPS

SUCCESSION SOWING

In my first season of GIYing, I sowed a full tray of over 50 lettuces – they were ready all at once, which would have been great had I been catering for a wedding… Succession sowing is one of the key skills I have learned as a GIYer. Rather than planting all at once, succession sowing is where you regularly sow a small amount of seeds to guarantee a continuous supply of your favourite vegetables. With some vegetables it makes sense to do a small sowing every three to four weeks, e.g. lettuce, oriental greens and annual spinach. Other vegetables have two to four sowings through the season, e.g. broad beans, peas, beetroot, calabrese, turnips, kohlrabi, leeks and kale.

LOOK AFTER BROAD BEANS

As soon as beans appear at the base of your broad bean plants you can 'pinch out' the growing tips which encourages the plant to focus on bean production rather than growing any taller. It also is said to prevent blackfly. The growing tip is at the very top of the plant - remove the tip with two leaves attached. You can eat these incidentally! I don't necessarily think you need to stake broad beans outside – the ones grown outside are generally quite hardy and won't fall over. If you have a windy site or if they appear to be falling over, you can put four small posts or bamboos around the broad bean bed and put a few lengths of string or twine around the posts. This will keep the plants from falling over.

GARLIC SPRAY

Here's a useful recipe for a disinfectant, anti-fungal garlic spray, which prevents pests from landing on plants (they don't like the smell of garlic) and enhances plant vigour. It can be used to spray tomatoes, peppers, aubergines, pumpkins, courgettes, basil etc., and even on brassicas to guard against cabbage white butterfly. Add three crushed cloves of garlic to a tablespoon of vegetable oil and leave to soak overnight. Strain the mixture and add one teaspoon liquid soap (hand soap or washing up liquid) and one litre of water. Put it in a spray bottle and shake well. Spray plants liberally once a week.

GROW MARIGOLDS

Marigolds are a great flower to grow, look beautiful and are also one of the most useful companion plants to have in your veggie patch. They give off a strong smell that will deter most aphids and greenfly. Dot them around your tomato plants and you will have far fewer problems with pests. They self-seed too - we have marigolds come up spontaneously in our polytunnel having being introduced a few years ago. Apparently it's a good idea to have them at the entrance to your polytunnel or greenhouse as it will keep aphids out altogether. The flowers of many varieties of marigold are edible too.

Gratin of Potatoes, Coolea Cheese and Wild Garlic

RORY O CONNELL

Coolea farmhouse cheese is a Gouda type cheese made in West Cork. Rich, buttery and nutty, it is delicious and a wheel in its entirety is magnificent. It is one of my favourite cheeses. The mature cheeses are wonderful as a dessert cheese and I sometimes, as here, use the younger cheeses in a gratin. You can happily replace the Coolea with gruyere. The wild garlic, a seasonal treat, can be replaced very successfully with spring onions. This flavoursome dish is excellent with roast and grilled meats.

SERVES 6

1.5kg potatoes, peeled

2 bunches of wild garlic leaves, finely chopped

10g butter

170g Coolea cheese, coarsely grated

450ml chicken stock

salt and pepper

From *Master It* by Rory O'Connell. Published by Fourth Estate 2013.

Preheat the oven to 200°C / 400°F / gas 6.

Slice the peeled potatoes 2mm thick. Bring a saucepan of water to the boil and add the sliced potatoes and stir gently to separate the slices of potato. Bring back to the boil and immediately strain and run the potatoes under a cold tap to cool down. Place the cooled and strained potato slices on a clean tea towel to drain further. Dab them dry. Smear an ovenproof gratin dish with half of the butter. Sprinkle with half of the wild garlic, one third of the potatoes and some grated cheese. Season with salt and pepper. Repeat this process again. Finish with a layer of the potatoes, neatly arranged. Pour over the boiling stock and scatter the remaining cheese over the top.

Bake for 1- 1 ¼ hours or until the potatoes are tender and the top is crispy and golden.

Serve with grilled lamb or chicken.

Nettle Soup with Wild Garlic Oil

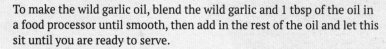

SERVES 4

1 tbsp olive oil, plus extra for drizzling

1 leek, washed and finely sliced

1 large floury potato (Maris Piper or similar), thinly sliced

1 litre vegetable stock

400g stinging or dead nettles, washed, leaves picked

50g butter, diced

50ml double cream

WILD GARLIC OIL

75g wild garlic

150ml extra virgin olive oil or Irish rapeseed oil

From Donal Skehan www.donalskehan.com

To make the wild garlic oil, blend the wild garlic and 1 tbsp of the oil in a food processor until smooth, then add in the rest of the oil and let this sit until you are ready to serve.

In a large saucepan, heat the oil over medium heat, stir in the leek and potato and cook for about 10 minutes, until the leek is soft.

Add in the stock and cook for another 10 minutes until the potato is soft. Now it's time to add in the nettles, simmer for a minute or two and then, using a hand-held mixer, blend the soup to a smooth consistency. Stir in the butter and cream and season with salt and pepper to taste.

Drizzle the wild garlic oil over each serving and serve with some nice sourdough bread.

Broad Bean Hummous – Crema di Fave

CATHERINE FULVIO

This is so tasty and healthy. I stir the leftovers into a pasta salad with rocket. It's ideal for those moments when unexpected visitors call by in the summer. Keeping it local: No need to shop locally, as the broad beans grow so easily in the garden – you don't have to be too 'green fingered', honestly! Local rapeseed oil is delicious in hummus. Try Second Nature rapeseed oil from Kilkenny.

MAKES ABOUT 250G

250g broad beans

5 tbsp extra virgin olive oil

2 garlic cloves, sliced

1 lemon, zest and juice

1 tbsp chopped parsley

salt and freshly ground black pepper

celery sticks, radishes and breadsticks for dipping.

From *Eat like an Italian* by Catherine Fulvio. Published by Gill & Macmillan 2012.

Boil the broad beans in rapidly boiling water for about 10 minutes, until tender. Drain and set aside.

Heat the olive oil in a small saucepan over a low heat. Add the garlic and simmer for a few minutes, taking care not to let the garlic burn.

Place the broad beans in a food processor. Add the garlic, oil, lemon zest and juice and process until fairly smooth. Add the parsley and season to taste.

Wild Garlic Pesto

DARINA ALLEN

We make this gorgeous pesto from April to mid-May. It's also good over salad leaves, goat's cheese, bruschetta and pasta. Sprinkle the flowers over the finished dish as a garnish.

MAKES 2 X 225 G (7FL OZ) JARS

50g (2oz) wild garlic leaves

25g (1oz) pine nuts (taste to make sure they are not rancid)

1 garlic clove, peeled and crushed

170-225ml (6-8fl oz olive oil)

40g (1 ½ oz Parmesan cheese, finely grated

salt and sugar to taste

From *Forgotten Skills of Cooking* by Darina Allen. Published by Kyle Cathie 2009.

Whizz the wild garlic leaves, pine nuts, garlic and olive oil in a food-processor or pound together in a pestle and mortar. Remove to a bowl and fold in the grated Parmesan. Taste and season. Store in a sterilised covered jar in the fridge.

Clean the top and sides of the jar each time you dip in. Cover with a layer of extra virgin olive oil and the lid of the jar. Pesto also freezes well, but for best results don't add the grated Parmesan until it has defrosted. Freeze in small amounts for convenience.

Gubbeen and Wild Sea Beet Pizza with Sea Grass

SALLY MCKENNA

SERVES 6

PIZZA DOUGH

500g strong white flour

10g dried yeast

1 teaspoon salt

350ml water

2 tablespoons olive oil

TOPPING

olive oil

sea beet leaves

Gubbeen cheese (you can also use Durrus, or any of the other semi-soft cheeses)

nutmeg

sea grass

From *Extreme Greens* by Sally McKenna. Published by Estragon Press, 2013.

Combine the flour, yeast and salt in a bowl. Mix in the water, and bring together to make a dough. Knead the dough for 10 minutes. This kneading can be done in various mixers, processors or in a bread machine.

Allow the dough to rise for about 2 hours, then shape into 6 balls of dough.

Preheat the oven to its hottest temperature.

Take each ball at a time and first press into a circle, then roll out thinly. Using a pizza peel, or your fingers, place on a hot oven tray. Rub the surface quickly with a little olive oil and scatter over the raw sea beet leaves (you can substitute spinach if unable to gather sea beet). Top with slices of cheese, and then sprinkle over the sea grass, and a generous grating of nutmeg.

Cook in a hot oven (as hot as it will go) for approximately 5-7 minutes. Serve straight from the oven.

Basil Pesto

DERVAL O ROURKE

Basil pesto is super-tasty and this is quite a healthy version. It can be enjoyed in sandwiches, as a dip or spread or as a sauce for pasta. You can use Parmesan, Pecorino or Grana Padano – whatever's available. Remember that cheese goes a long way in pesto, so if you're looking for an even healthier version you could reduce the quantity of cheese by half.

MAKES A SMALL JAR

1 whole fresh basil plant, leaves picked and washed but not dried

40g Parmesan, grated

40g shelled pistachios

2 cloves garlic, peeled

2 tbsp olive oil

2 tbsp water

1 tbsp extra virgin olive oil

½ tsp sea salt

a pinch of black pepper

From *Food for the Fast Lane: Recipes to Power Your Body and Mind* by Derval O'Rourke. Published by Gill & Macmillan 2014.

Place all of the ingredients in a large mixing bowl and use a handblender to blitz until the pesto reaches your desired consistency.

This pesto will keep in a jam jar in the fridge for up to ten days. Just make sure you pour a thin film of olive oil over the top of the pesto before you put the lid on – this will seal in the flavour and keep the pesto from darkening.

Rhubarb and Ginger Jam

ALYS FOWLER

This recipe is a favourite in many old jam books. I adapted it slightly by adding some cinnamon and a little orange juice.

2kg rhubarb, cut into 2cm chunks

1.75-2kg light brown sugar

100g chopped crystallised ginger (grated fresh ginger could be used instead but you might need to add more sugar)

225ml orange juice

1 small cinnamon stick

juice of 2 lemons (or 1 level teaspoon citric acid)

sterilised jam jars with lids – how many you need depends on the size of your jars.

From *Abundance* by Alys Fowler.
Published by Kyle Books 2013

Wash and dry the rhubarb, layer it up with the sugar in a large non-reactive bowl, cover with a tea-towel and set aside to macerate somewhere cool overnight.

The following morning, most of the sugar will be dissolved and the rhubarb will be sitting in it's own juices.

Tip the contents of the bowl into a preserving pan, add the ginger, orange juice, cinnamon stick and lemon juice (or citric acid) and slowly bring to the boil, stirring. Boil rapidly until the rhubarb is tender and the jam reaches setting point, about 30 minutes. Pour into warm sterilised jars and seal.

June

IT'S HARD TO BELIEVE THAT we're now in the sixth month of the year already, and that the longest day of the year is a mere three weeks away. What I consider my "big 7" direct-sow sowings – garlic, potatoes, broad beans, peas, onions, carrots and parsnips - are now complete. Of course there is still lots of sowing to do (right up until August or September) but there is a definite sense of completion, if not finality, in the air.

I am doing a lot of transplanting at the moment, which is always a fun activity for a GIYer. There's nothing like the satisfaction of planting seedlings – bare beds transformed in an instant with neat rows of little plants. I love how suddenly the veg patch is transformed from bare to almost-full in June. I always feel intensely happy after spending some time planting – and now I know that there is actually a scientific reason for this: contact with soil triggers the release of serotonin in our brain according to research. Serotonin is the happy chemical – it is a natural anti-depressant and strengthens the immune system.

On the other hand, there are always a few days of fretting after transplanting– will cold nights set the plants back? Will slugs or rabbits try and munch on them? Planting a seedling out in the soil therefore is a watershed moment. It is the moment it leaves a very controlled environment in favour of something far more uncontrolled, unpredictable and messy. And like a parent sending a child off to school for the first time, you just have to have faith and let it go in to the mad, bad world!!

Left: *The veg patch in June.*

THIS MONTH'S TOP JOBS

* Monthly indoor sowing of lettuce, oriental greens, annual spinach, calabrese, coriander.

* Sow indoors: winter cabbage, purple sprouting broccoli, fennel (2), kale (2), perpetual spinach (2), Swiss chard (2), kohlrabi (3), scallions (2).

* Net soft fruits like strawberries against birds.

* Direct strawberry runners in to pots of compost to provide new plants for next year's growing.

* Harvest winter garlic.

Things to Do in... *June*

PREP WORK AND TO DO LIST

Watering and weeding duties step up a notch – the tunnel/
greenhouse in particular will require a good deal of water from
now on. Watch the weather and water outside as required.
Water in the morning if possible. Add a good dressing of mulch
around plants to reduce moisture loss and keep down weeds.
Continue to earth-up potato plants to prevent the spuds
becoming green. It's time to get really seriously vigilant with
your tomato plants – mulch, water and continue to remove
side shoots that appear in the leaf axils. Train the plants
carefully on strings or strong canes.

Below: *A
meitheal at
WLRFM in
Waterford*

   If gooseberry and red current bushes are very leafy, start
summer pruning by shortening back the new growth. Tie up
beans and peas to stop them falling over – mature pea plants
become like a canopy and could take off in the wind, bound for
next door's garden. Stake everything that grows tall –
raspberries, peas, beans etc. Net soft fruit against birds – it's
worth the effort. They are far more vigilant than we are, and
will eat your entire crop practically overnight if you let them.

SOWING SEEDS

In addition to your monthly sowing of leaves, sow indoors:
winter cabbage, purple sprouting broccoli, fennel (2), kale (2),
perpetual spinach (2), Swiss chard (2), kohlrabi (3), scallions (2).
Sow Parsley now to provide a late supply in autumn and some
of the plants can then be lifted, potted and brought indoors for
winter use.

PLANTING OUT

It's time to plant out pretty much anything else which has been raised indoors or undercover and needs transplanting, e.g. leeks, Brussels sprouts, cabbage, cauliflower, celery, celeriac, cucumbers, pumpkin, courgettes, squash, runner beans, climbing French beans etc.

HARVESTING – WHAT'S IN SEASON?

June is a busy month for the GIYer but it's also (thankfully) the month when we really start to see some payback - the first broad beans and peas as well as new potatoes, beetroot and carrots from the polytunnel, and fruit like gooseberries, cherries and strawberries. You may even see the first tomato. Herbs are in full flow. This month you might also be harvesting kohlrabi, cabbage, cauliflower (month end), spinach, spring onion, salad leaves, elderflower, rhubarb, garlic and sea-kale.

Top left: *GIY photo boards at Bloom 2014. When classic art meets GIY!*

Bottom left: *Aaron, Feargal and myself - two great members of Waterford GIY - the first ever GIY group!*

Veg of the Month - *Peas*

WHY GROW THEM?

Peas are almost never available in the shops fresh, always frozen. As soon as a pea is picked from the plant the sugars inside it start to turn to starch which means the flavour starts to deteriorate immediately. So, peas that are cooked immediately after picking will always taste nicer than the frozen alternative. Kids love 'em. My kids are the greatest threat to our fresh peas – they move up and down the rows picking and eating peas like two mini-hoovers.

SOWING

Peas can be sown direct in the soil, or in module trays for later transplanting. I always sow them direct. If sowing direct in the soil, make sure the temperature is consistently above 10 degrees celsius. Dig a trench 15cm wide and 4cm deep and place the peas on the surface in two staggered rows at least 5cm apart. You can enjoy fresh peas from May to October if you 'succession sow' (do at least two sowings – late March and late May).

GROWING

Peas are hungry plants - dig in well-rotted manure or compost the previous winter and apply a good quality organic fertiliser just before sowing. Once they get going however you won't need to feed them as peas are nitrogen "fixers" – they can take nitrogen from the air. Peas need support and it's more effective to get the support in place when sowing as opposed to trying to do it later when the plants are established. An effective support is to run lengths of chicken wire between posts with rows of peas on either side. You can also use "peasticks" (lengths of hazel). Pea plants send out little tendrils that grasp at anything they can find for support – I've always wondered how they "know" where to grasp?! Water the plants well when they are flowering, if it's dry outside.

HARVESTING

Peas are usually ready to harvest about 3-4 months after sowing. Harvest regularly to encourage pod production. Pinch off the growing tip of the plants when the first pods are ready – this will encourage the plant to focus on pod production. The growing tips and leaves of the pea plant are edible and a very tasty addition to a salad. Most peas are taken from the pods to eat, but with mangetout and sugar snap peas the whole pod is eaten. Once the plant is finished cut it down but leave the roots in the soil – the nitrogen that the plant has taken from the air is "fixed" in the soil.

GIY RECOMMENDED VARIETIES

Onward, Meteor, Ambassador, Rondo.

PROBLEMS

Peas can get powdery mildew in the summer which appears on leaves – use resistant varieties.

GIY TIPS

- Peas can be sown effectively in lengths of old rain-guttering. Fill the gutter with potting compost and sow seeds 5cm apart. When the seedlings are 8cm tall dig a trench in the soil about the same depth as the compost in the gutter and simply slide out the contents of the gutter in to the trench.
- Many GIYers grow peas just to eat the growing tips of the young plants which are a trendy delicacy and look great in salads. If growing them this way, sow them very close together in a seed tray and simply snip off the top of the plants with a scissors when they are about 15cm tall.

FORAGING

Bringing freshly picked food to the table doesn't always have to involve sowing and growing it yourself. Sometimes, happily, you can allow nature to do the hard work for you. Free, wild food is abundant in hedgerows and trees, on beaches, in woodland, hillsides and even in your garden - all you really need to know is what to look for and when to look for it.

Wild garlic – you know it's spring when the first wild garlic appears (early March). Grows best in woodlands and is fantastic for salad, pesto, and to flavour soups, stews and pies. Wild garlic pesto freezes well so can be used as a way to "store" it if you have a lot – given how abundantly it grows that's very likely.

Elderflower –I always think that elder is a great starter for novice foragers because it's so easy to identify. The biggest clue is that the flowers are cream, not white. They also have an unmistakably earthy, almost musty, aroma. The season for elderflower is short – about six weeks or so in late May and June. Each year I try and forage a batch to make cordials and champagne.

Seaweed – if you're lucky enough to live by the seashore, there are an abundance of foraging options through the year. Seaweed is really the holy grail for veg patch fertility (to cover beds in winter as an alternative to farmyard manure or compost) and of course has a whole range of culinary and health benefits too.

Nettles – Spring nettles (at their best when young – from February on) have all manner of health benefits: high in vitamins and minerals, blood-cleansing, anti-bacterial, anti-inflammatory, anti-allergy. A tea made from nettles (really an infusion) is a super tonic, or you could try making a nettle soup. Nettle tea has a rich and earthy taste that won't appeal to everyone but you can sweeten with some honey. Also a brilliant liquid fertiliser for your garden when soaked in water.

Blackberries – the hedgerow around our garden is laden down with fruit in the late summer and autumn (August and September). I've always found it fascinating that nature loads hedges with fruit that's packed with Vitamin C just as we're heading in to the cold winter months. Equally bizarre is the fact that gazillions of blackberries rot on the hedges in the countryside while people spend €8 on a punnet of blueberries in the supermarkets. Get out there with some kids, some buckets and get picking!

Mushrooms – the only time I've ever felt safe picking and eating mushrooms is on a mushroom foraging expedition led by an expert. Apparently, more people die from mushroom hunting than from extreme sports, which I guess means that mushroom foraging can be considered an extreme sport in itself. Picture two mushrooms side by side – one can be a delicious dinner (chanterelle, field mushrooms etc.), the other could kill you. And sometimes they look the same. So, never eat a wild mushroom unless it has been identified as safe to eat by an expert.

Other foraging options – **dandelion root and leaf**, **crab apples**, **samphire**, **sorrel**, **wild strawberries**, **rose hips** and **sloe**.

WILD GARLIC

ELDERFLOWER

SEAWEED

NETTLES

BLACKBERRIES

MUSHROOMS

JUNE TIPS

EARTHING UP

As your potato plants grow, you need to "earth them up" - this is a process of drawing soil up around the plant's stems to cover them. It increases the length of underground "potato bearing" stem so that you end up with more spuds per plant. It also stops potatoes from poking through the soil, which would cause them to go green. I use a tool called a ridging hoe, which looks like something the Grim Reaper would sling over his shoulder – walking along the row, I use the hoe like a scythe, drawing soil up around the potato plants to cover about half of the stem (10cm). It's a good plan to do this earlier in the season when the plants are small – it gets harder to do it effectively as the plants get taller.

MAKE YOUR OWN COMFREY OR NETTLE TEA

A nettle tea infusion is remarkable for your own health (see section on foraging), but did you know that nettles also make a great liquid fertiliser for your plants? Chop fresh nettle stems and pack them in to a bucket, covering with water. Cover with a stone or slab to keep the nettles submerged in the water. Leave it for 2-3 weeks. The resulting feed will smell foul, but is dynamite for plants as it's full of nutrients. To use, dilute ten parts water to one part nettle feed. This will be particularly beneficial for leafy plants such as brassicas since it's nitrogen rich. Fruiting crops like tomatoes will benefit more from a potassium rich feed like that made from comfrey. The process (and dilution rate) is the same to make comfrey tea.

KNOWING WHEN TO HARVEST GARLIC

Knowing when to lift garlic can be a tricky proposition - harvest them too early and the bulbs will be too small, but harvest too late and the bulbs will begin to lose their quality. The old rule is to sow garlic before the shortest day of the year (December 21st) and harvest before the longest (June 21st). Some people (including me) sow garlic in spring instead, which won't be ready until late July or August. A good general rule of thumb is to do a test when a third of the leaves on each plant are gone brown. Carefully push back the soil around one plant and have a look at the bulb to check its size. If it's too small, put the soil back around it and leave them alone for another week or so. Lift all your garlic when a half to two-thirds of the leaves are gone brown.

PLANT OUT COURGETTE, SQUASH AND PUMPKIN

We're at the stage now where it's time to plant out courgette, squash and pumpkin plants. The key when planting them out is to dig a decent sized hole (about 12 inches wide and deep - i.e. a spades depth) and fill it with a mix of good quality, well-rotted compost/manure and soil. Fill it so that there is a mound on the surface of the soil. Sow the plant in the mound and then water in well. Slug control is crucial until the plant gets established. Also very important to keep the soil around the plants moist - water copiously around the plants, not over them. Once it starts to fruit, feed every two weeks with tomato feed or comfrey/nettle tea.

DIY 'Pot' Noodle

HUGH FEARNLEY WHITTINGSTALL

I first experimented with these when I was looking at ways to improve workday lunches. However, the concept works equally well as a fast and very satisfying supper. It's important to find the right kind of noodle – one that will soften nicely in boiling water from the kettle without the need for pan-cooking. I find flat, thin, quick-cook egg noodles fit the bill very well. The 'pot' should be covered once the water is added... with this in mind, a sealable heatproof jar, such as a kilner, is ideal.

SERVES 1

1 nest of thin, quick-cook egg noodles

1 teaspoon vegetable bouillon powder, or ¼ veg stock cube

a good pinch of soft brown sugar

1 small carrot, peeled and very thinly sliced or cut into fine julienne

3–4 spring onions, trimmed and finely sliced

6 sugar snap peas, shredded, or a few frozen petits pois

1 leaf of spring greens or green cabbage or a couple of leaves of pak choi, stalk removed, finely shredded

½ teaspoon freshly grated ginger

½ garlic clove, grated

¼ red or green chilli, deseeded and finely chopped

2 teaspoons soy sauce

juice of ½ lime

From *River Cottage Veg Every Day* by Hugh Fearnley-Whittingstall. Published by Bloomsbury 2011.

Put all the ingredients, except the soy sauce and lime, in a 'pot'. Pour over boiling water to just cover everything, pressing the ingredients down. Cover and leave for 8–10 minutes, stirring once or twice, then add soy sauce and lime juice to taste, and eat.

VARIATION

Curried mushroom pot. This works 'instantly' with raw mushrooms and defrosted frozen peas; you can of course add other finely sliced or shredded cooked veg too. Mix ½ teaspoon cornflour with 1 teaspoon curry powder and put into a 'pot' with a nest of thin, quick-cook egg noodles, 3–4 finely sliced mushrooms, 1 tablespoon defrosted frozen peas, 1 finely grated small garlic clove and a finely grated 1–2cm piece of ginger, along with about 25g paneer (Indian cheese) if you can get hold of some. Season with salt and pepper. Pour over boiling water to just cover everything, pressing the ingredients down. Cover and leave for 8–10 minutes, stirring once or twice, then eat.

Chickpeas with Spinach, Red Onion, Roast Cumin, Tomatoes and Lemon

RORY O'CONNELL

This is a simple dish which can be enjoyed with rice for a vegetarian supper and also makes a lovely accompaniment for roast or grilled lamb or pork. The dish, which should be rich in flavour and juicy, reheats perfectly, so can if necessary be prepared ahead of time. Always remember to keep some of the liquid drained off the cooked pulses. It may be needed to loosen out the sauce if it is too thick, or to add a little more liquid when reheating. Pulse dishes like this sometimes need robust seasoning, so don't be too polite with it. If it seems a little dull, add another pinch of salt and sugar for the tomatoes. If it is a little watery, just allow it to bubble with the lid off for a few minutes longer. If you have a little left over it freezes quite well.

SERVES 4 AS A MAIN DISH OR 8 AS AN ACCOMPANIMENT

190g dried chickpeas, soaked overnight in 1 litre of cold water

600g spinach

2 tablespoons olive oil

2 medium red onions, peeled and finely diced

2 cloves of garlic, peeled and thinly sliced

400g ripe tomatoes peeled and chopped or same weight of tinned or bottled tomatoes

1 teaspoon of cumin seeds, roasted and coarsely ground

grated zest of 1 lemon

Master It by Rory O'Connell. Published by Fourth Estate 2013.

Drain the chickpeas and discard the soaking water. Rinse the chickpeas under a cold tap and place in a clean saucepan with 1 litre of fresh water. Bring to a boil, reduce the heat to a simmer, cover and cook for about 1 hour until tender. When tender, drain the cooking water and reserve.

Remove the stalks from the spinach and slice the stalks finely across the grain. Rinse the leaves and allow to drain.

Heat the olive oil in a wide low-sided saucepan or sauté pan and add the sliced garlic. Allow to turn just golden and immediately add the ground cumin seed, diced onions and spinach stalks. Season with salt and pepper, stir to mix and cover the pan. Lower the heat and allow to cook very gently until the onions are tender. This takes about 15 minutes. Remove the lid and add the tomatoes. Season with salt, pepper and a pinch of sugar. Allow to bubble up and cook covered at a simmer for 10 minutes or until the tomatoes have softened to a rich tomato sauce.

Turn the heat up and add the spinach leaves. You will have to work a little when adding the leaves, but gradually they will wilt down and fit in the pan. Cook until the spinach is just collapsed and tender.

Add the drained cooked chickpeas, and a little of the cooking liquid if the mixture looks a little dry. The mixture should be juicy. Allow to simmer for 5 minutes. Taste and correct seasoning. Sometimes a pinch of sugar can transform the dish and remember that chickpeas need plenty of seasoning.

Serve in a large warmed serving dish, sprinkled with the lemon zest.

Nettle and Chive Champ

BIDDY WHITE LENNON

As a food grower and cook I treasure nettles for the compost heap and the pot. Nettles, if harvested regularly, will grow again and provide fresh leaves from early spring to autumn. The tender tops are for the pot and the rest for the compost heap or for plant feeding. Nettles were eaten as a spring tonic either as nettle tea, in 'potato and nettle soup', or in the Northeast and Northwest of Ireland, mixed into this traditional potato dish.

SERVES 4-6

800g floury potatoes, washed

4 scallions

about 200ml hot milk

about 100g fresh tender nettle tops

about 60g butter

chives to taste

sea salt and freshly ground black pepper

From Biddy White Lennon
www.biddywhitelennon.com

Using gloves strip nettle leaves from stalk and blanch in fast boiling water for a few minutes. Drain and chop finely. Clean and chop scallion. Melt a little butter in a small pan and soften for a minute. Snip chives.

Steam potatoes until tender. Lift steamer from pot and dry off by placing a tea towel on top for a few minutes. While still hot, peel and then put through a food mill or potato ricer.

Mix in the hot milk, blanched nettle tops, scallions, snipped chives and butter. Season with salt and pepper to taste. Serve piping hot. I have found it can be reheated in a microwave and any leftovers make great potato cakes.

Pea, Mint & Roast Garlic Soup

DOMINI KEMP

Unless I'm in the heart of gazpacho territory in Spain, the idea of cold soups sends a shiver of ickiness down my spine. I get the same feeling when I'm served a main course of fish with vegetable ice cream as a garnish. This chilled pea soup, however, is a delight. You can make it with frozen peas, which, along with frozen broad beans and soy beans, have to be one of the world's handiest frozen foods. You can, of course, use fresh peas, but I find them rather inconsistent and sometimes downright horrible when bought in a supermarket, as they're invariably flown in from Kenya or somewhere far, far away. If you can't grow them yourself, frozen peas are a really great product. Serve this up in glasses as a posh starter or just enjoy a bowl of it, undisturbed, with some nice bread on a sunny day. You could also garnish this with a few peas and some small pieces of diced chorizo, which you can fry in a little oil.

SERVES 4-6

2 to 3 tbsp olive oil

1 head garlic, broken into unpeeled cloves

a few sprigs of thyme

salt and freshly ground black pepper

a knob of butter

1 kg homegrown or frozen peas

1 litre water

a handful of mint

200ml cream or crème fraîche

From *Itsa Cookbook* by Domini Kemp. Published by Gill & Macmillan 2010.

Heat the olive oil in a small saucepan. Poach the garlic cloves, thyme and a little salt and pepper, covered, for 5 to 10 minutes on a very gentle heat, until just soft. Cooking the garlic this way makes it utterly addictive, but be sure to keep the heat very gentle and to cover the saucepan with a lid, because if the garlic burns, it will taste rotten. Allow to cool fully.

Heat the butter in a large saucepan, add the frozen peas and chuck in the water. Cook until the peas have just thawed. Squeeze the garlic flesh from their skins into the peas and add the mint. Blitz with a hand-held immersion blender or else do it in batches in your blender or food processor until smooth.

Pour into a bowl, add cream to taste and season well. Chill until ready to serve. It lasted a few days in my fridge and didn't lose its gorgeous Shrek-like green colour, but it will taste better if eaten within 24 hours.

Elderflower and Gooseberry Fool

LILLY HIGGINS

Place the gooseberries in a saucepan and pour over the cordial. Simmer and poach the berries in the cordial for 4-5 minutes, until they burst. Allow to cool.

In a separate bowl, whip the cream until it's thick and voluminous, then fold in the yoghurt. Stir through half the poached gooseberries.

Line up 6 glasses and spoon some berries into the bottom of each glass. Top with the cream and continue to layer and swirl the cream and berries together. Cover and place in the fridge until ready to serve.

Top with a light scattering of elderflower petals.

SERVES 6

1kg gooseberries

250ml elderflower cordial

400ml cream

150ml Greek yoghurt

elderflower petals, to decorate

From *Dream Deli* by Lilly Higgins.
Published by Gill & Macmillan, 2013.

Elderflower Champagne

ALYS FOWLER

Elderflower champagne is a wonderful drink –
so easy, cheap and delicious.

4.5 litres (8pints) water

650g (1¼lb) white sugar

6-8 elderflower heads, fully
open (the largest you can
find)

2 unwaxed lemons

2 tablespoons white wine
vinegar

a packet of champagne
yeast or a dessertspoon
of dried yeast (not always
necessary)

a scrupulously clean 15 litre
(2 gallon) bucket with a lid

From *The Thrifty Forager* by Alys Fowler
Published by Kyle Books, 2011.

Boil roughly half the water and add the sugar, stirring until it is
completely dissolved. Allow this to cool.

Next add the elderflowers (give them a good shake first to dislodge any
insects or debris), squeeze in the lemon juice and chuck in the lemon
rind for good measure. Add the vinegar and the cooled water and cover
with a lid.

You need to leave this for 4 days to ferment, then you should start to see
bubbles and foam appearing. The process is temperature-dependent and
sometimes takes longer – if it's a little chilly, move it somewhere warmer.

If you don't see any fermentation after 4-5 days, add the yeast (the
benefit of using champagne yeast is that it ensures no rogue yeasts get
in which can cause the 'homebrew' hangover). If you've added yeast,
leave for another 4 days, by which time it really should bubble!

Next you need to strain out the flower heads and lemon rind, and bottle.

It is safe to say that elderflower champagne really fizzes and if you
use glass bottles, they will need to have swing tops (the type some
continental beers come in), but be warned these can sometimes
explode. I buy the cheapest supermarket value water in 2 litre plastic
bottles, use this in the recipe and bottle in these – rather than worrying
about the nice looking bottle. I'd rather actually have the champagne!
You can tell if the champagne is fizzing too much as the plastic bottle
will become rigid and sound hollow when tapped with a finger. Release
a little of the gas by unscrewing the top just a little.

After 10 days, your champagne should be ready to drink. It doesn't store
for long, about 6 weeks, but it's so good to drink I doubt that you'll have
any left.

Blackcurrant Lemon-Vanilla Verbena Glazed Tart with Cornmeal Crust

IMEN MCDONNELL

SERVES 6-8

CRUST

300g/2 ½ cups all purpose flour

30g/¼ cup corn (maize) meal (medium ground)

3 tablespoons sugar

¾ teaspoon salt

113g/½ cup plus 6 tablespoons chilled unsalted butter, cut into ½-inch cubes

55g/¼ cup nonhydrogenated solid vegetable shortening frozen, cut into ½-inch pieces

4 tablespoons (or more) icy water

GLAZE

2 teacups (or handfuls) washed fresh lemon verbena leaves

1 vanilla pod

450g/2 cups sugar

120ml/½ cup water

FILLING

750g/5 cups fresh blackcurrants (about 27 ounces)

175ml/¾ cup lemon verbena glaze

120g/½ cup caster sugar

30g/¼ cup cornstarch

milk (for brushing)

1 ½ tablespoon raw sugar

From Imen McDonnell, www.farmette.ie

FOR CRUST: Blend flour, cornmeal, sugar and salt in processor.

Add butter and shortening; blitz on and off until mixture resembles coarse meal. Add 4 tablespoons icy water and blend just until moist clumps begin to form. Gather dough into ball.

Divide dough in half; flatten each half into disk. Wrap disks separately in plastic and chill at least 1 hour.

FOR GLAZE: Put all ingredients into saucepan and slowly heat just until sugar dissolves and creates a thick syrup. Remove from heat and let cool and steep for 2 hours (or longer if you can, the longer you steep the more pronounced the flavour). Strain leaves and pod. Reserve syrup for glaze.

FOR FILLING: Combine black currants, lemon verbena glaze, sugar, cornstarch in large bowl; toss to blend. Let stand at room temperature until juices begin to form, about 30 minutes.

Preheat oven to 200°C/400°F. Place rimmed baking sheet in bottom of oven. Roll out 1 dough disk between 2 sheets of generously floured parchment paper to 12-inch round.

Peel off top parchment sheet; invert dough into 9-inch-diameter glass pie dish. Carefully peel off second parchment sheet.

Gently press dough into pie dish, pressing any cracks together as needed to seal and leaving dough overhang. Spoon filling into piecrust.

Roll out second dough disk between 2 sheets of generously floured parchment paper to 12-inch round.

Peel off top parchment sheet. Carefully and evenly invert dough atop filling. Peel off second parchment sheet. Trim overhang of both crusts to 1 inch. Fold overhang under and press to seal. Crimp edges.

Cut five 2-inch-long slits in top crust of pie to allow steam to escape during baking. Lightly brush top crust (not edges) with milk. Sprinkle with raw sugar.

Bake tart 15 minutes. Reduce oven temperature to 175°C/350°F and continue baking until crust is golden brown and filling is bubbling thickly through slits, about 1 hour 15 minutes.

Cool pie completely on rack. Serve with scoops of ice cream, custard, or whipped cream.

Top left: *Imen McDonnell and family.*

Sweet and Simple Strawberry Cupcakes

MARIAN KEYES

These are delicious little delights. Quick and easy to make, they come out super-light and airy and the fresh strawberries are a sweet surprise.

MAKES 12

200g fresh strawberries

100ml sunflower oil

90g caster sugar

2 eggs

180g plain flour

¾ teaspoon bicarbonate of soda

From *Saved by Cake* by Marian Keyes
Published by Michael Joseph 2012.

Preheat the oven to 180°C/350°F/gas 4 and line a 12-hole cupcake tray with paper or silicone cases. Wash and hull the strawberries and mash until they're pulpy.

Beat the oil, sugar and eggs together for a few minutes until the mix starts to look caramelly. Add the pulped strawberries, sieve in the flour and bicarbonate of soda and fold through. Pour the thinnish batter into the cases and bake for about 20 minutes. Cool on a wire rack and decorate pinkly.

July

DARE I SAY IT? THAT THINGS SEEM to have quietened down a little? I find myself standing in the vegetable patch and thinking – you know what, there's actually nothing more for me to do here. Go do something else. Play with your kids, go to the beach. Something other than GIYing.

So what's going on? Well, ironically, though the vegetable patch is resplendent and heaving with produce, July is one of those rare things – a month when there's not so much work to do. It's like we're in the eye of the storm – the worst has passed and the worst is perhaps yet to come, but for now, well it's peaceful and…almost a little eerie.

Weeding duties are not as severe as they were earlier in the season (at this stage of the year, you're either on top of them or you're not), and after a frenetic May and June, even the seed sowing has slowed down to a virtual stop. I'm doing some harvesting alright, but it's the "as you need it" type of harvesting rather than a major autumn harvesting job like onions or spuds. We don't even have massive gluts of produce that require processing (in to jams, chutneys, pickles or preserves) yet.

July is, to my mind, one of only two months in the entire year when I am freed from the gorgeous tyranny of the veggie patch (the other month is December). So I guess I should just kick back and enjoy it. Shouldn't I?

Left: Tomatoes ripening in polytunnel (note growbag experiment).

THIS MONTH'S TOP JOBS

* Monthly indoor sowing of lettuce, oriental greens, annual spinach, calabrese, coriander.

* Sow indoors: spring cabbage.

* Cover brassicas with netting to keep butterfly away.

* Start a bartering arrangement with fellow GIYers.

Things to Do in... *July*

PREP WORK AND TO DO LIST

Any ground that has finished cropping must be quickly cleared away to take more vegetables - this is the essence of a productive veggie patch. Write down your successes and failures – make a note of when things were sowed, transplanted, harvested etc. These records will be invaluable for next year. GIYers have great plans but poor memories! Use your produce - eat it, freeze it, process it, exchange it, give it away. Do not let it rot in the ground or end up on the compost heap. Continue to water and feed plants and practice good weed control. Continue to pinch out side shoots on your tomato plants and remove the lower leaves. Earth up brassicas such as Brussels sprouts - these plants will grow tall and require a good deal of support. Prune raspberries and gooseberries when they have finished fruiting and apply a mulch. Cut down legume plants that have finished cropping and compost them. Leave the roots in the soil as they fix nitrogen in the soil. At the first signs of blight on potato leaves, cut down stalks at ground level to prevent blight travelling to the tubers – at this time of the year, the spuds should be big enough to still represent a decent crop. Don't be tempted to spray – whatever chemicals you spray on plants, end up on the kitchen table and in your stomach eventually…!

SOWING SEEDS

Continue successional sowings and use quick maturing varieties for autumn use - Swiss chard, lettuce, oriental greens,

Quackers about ducks!

The joy of homegrown toms – diversity of shapes, colours and sizes.

rocket, salad onions, radish and white turnips. Sow for winter use (yes you read that correctly – it's time to start thinking about growing things that will crop in winter) - spring cabbage, Hungry Gap kale, parsley, perpetual spinach and coriander.

PLANTING OUT

Plant out anything left in pots or trays.

HARVESTING – WHAT'S IN SEASON?

July is a peak month for produce – enjoy it! Pick early and often as some vegetables stop producing if not continually picked. First crops of French and runner beans, tomatoes, peppers, cucumbers, courgette and aubergine, beetroot, globe artichokes. Continue to harvest new potatoes, calabrese, cauliflower, cabbage, spinach, carrots, turnips, shallots, garlic, radish, spring onions, salad crops, strawberries, raspberries, tayberries, currants (black, red and white), gooseberries, loganberries, peas, broad beans. Ask yourself – do you really need to go to the supermarket?!

Left: *Glut city – courgette and cucumber overload.*

 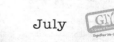

Veg of the Month - *Courgette*

WHY GROW IT?

They are easy to grow and incredibly prolific, growing freakishly fast in the summer. Two or three plants will be more than enough. Your only problem in fact will be working out what to do with all those courgettes. After I have exhausted all my courgette recipes - courgette cake, courgette bread etc. – I often resort to going to visit friends, family and neighbours, bearing 'gifts' of bag loads of courgettes…

SOWING

Sow seeds indoors in pots at a depth of 2cm from April. They will need temperatures of 20 degrees celsius to germinate so leave the pots on a sunny windowsill. Harden off well and transplant in June. Don't be fooled by their size when you are first planting the seedlings out. Courgettes grow to large, hungry and thirsty plants so leave a minimum of 70-100cm between plants. Dig plenty of well rotted compost in to the soil before transplanting.

GROWING

Never let the soil dry out – use a mulch around the plants to preserve moisture. They will need lots of water particularly when the courgettes are starting to swell. If you have added plenty of manure when planting, they shouldn't need feeding, but if you think the growth is slow use a general purpose organic fertiliser, or make your own comfrey tea. Courgette plants have male and female flowers on the same plant and insects will generally carry pollen from one to the other at which point the female flower starts to become a fruit. If the plants are grown under cover, you may have to pollinate them by hand. Admittedly, I've never tried that.

HARVESTING

Harvest regularly when the courgettes are about pencil length. They are at their best at this stage, and quickly become watery and relatively tasteless thereafter. The more you pick the more fruit the plant will produce. Don't leave big marrow-sized courgettes on the plant, as it will reduce the production of new fruits.

GIY RECOMMENDED VARIETIES

Genovese, Cocozelle, Ambassador.

PROBLEMS

Powdery mildew is the most common problem and appears as a white powder on leaves at the end of the summer. It is not a huge issue and mainly just affects the leaves. Slugs are an issue for newly planted seedlings – protect them carefully!

GIY TIPS

- I know a GIYer who freezes sliced courgettes for use in the winter as a filler/bulking agent for soups and stews.
- Allow at least some of your courgettes to grow in to giant marrows at the end of the season – then pick and store them. The thick skin will preserve them over the winter.

MONTHLY INSIGHT– CONTAINER GROWING

5 TIPS FOR GROWING INDOORS

1 A windowsill indoors is a great substitute for a greenhouse/polytunnel, and is an ideal location for raising seedlings.

2 Most herbs will do very well indoors in small containers and it's ideal to have them so close to the kitchen.

3 Try growing sprouting seeds such as mustard, chickpeas and fenugreek – they make an excellent addition to salads or a great, healthy snack, and they don't need much space.

4 Peppers (chilli and sweet) are compact little plants and like heat and light and so will do very well indoors.

5 Dwarf varieties of vegetables are ideal for growing indoors. Try dwarf varieties of peas, beans, tomatoes, aubergines and cabbages.

APARTMENT BALCONY GROWING

- With a bit of ingenuity an apartment balcony can be turned in to your very own GROW HQ.
- The key to maximising growing space is to go vertical! Each shelf on a four or five-shelf plastic "greenhouse" will support about five pots.
- Work out which part of your balcony gets the most sunlight. Some plants need direct sunlight while others will tolerate or prefer partial shade. Lettuce is an example of a plant that enjoys some shade.
- Use existing balcony features such as a railing to trail climbing plants up. You can also hang rectangular planters from the rails.
- Your veggies may be exposed to the elements if you are growing high up on a balcony, so use netting or bamboo screens to act as a windbreak. You may also need to water more if rain doesn't get in to the balcony.
- On the flipside, slugs and other pests are rarely a problem on an apartment balcony! Slugs are persistent but as far as I know, they are not so persistent that they would scale an apartment building in search of their supper.

JULY TIPS

USING SPACE

At this time of the year, you can use space made available by harvesting to plant up quick growing vegetables such as oriental greens, or turnips (white turnips, not swedes), radish, annual spinach, or lettuce. Another option is if a few old tubers of seed sized potatoes (size of an egg) are on hand, these may be planted, early to mid-July, to have new potatoes available in the early winter.

SOW A GREEN MANURE

A good way to use available space in the veggie patch is to sow 'green manures' such as mustard, buckwheat, radish, rye, alfalfa, clover and vetches. Green manures are plants which are grown specifically to improve soil fertility and useful at times when beds are empty (as is often the case in summer). Grow directly in the bed and then cut down and dig in to the soil, improving the soil structure and nutrient level as well as preventing the leaching of nutrients. Some also have very pretty flowers and will attract bees and other beneficial insects.

MAKE YOUR OWN RIBENA

Here's a recipe to deal with those gluts of blackcurrants. This makes about 750ml of a lovely ribena-type drink that will keep for 3 weeks in the fridge. You can also freeze it in ice-cube trays and then just pop a few cubes in a glass when you need a drink. De-stalk and wash 450g blackcurrants. Place them in a saucepan with 250g caster sugar and 260ml water. Over a low heat, melt the sugar, stirring

occasionally. Bring the syrup to a gentle boil and simmer for 5 minutes. Add the juice and zest of 1 lemon. Simmer for another 5 minutes. Allow to cool and then pour in to a sterilised bottle through a fine sieve. Dilute to taste. Yum.

LOOK AFTER RUNNER BEANS

Loosely tie the plants to supports to start but after that they should climb themselves quite happily. Water plants copiously during dry weather to maximise pod development. Pinch off the growing tip once the plants have reached the top of their supports (about 8ft). Mulch around stems to preserve moisture and keep weeds down. Don't forget to succession sow - you could have a second, much later crop of beans in October, if you sow some seeds now.

EARTH UP LEEKS

A good leek (from a culinary perspective) has got a substantial amount of white flesh and a short green top. The key to getting this is to "earth up" leeks at this time of the year to encourage blanching or bleaching of the stems (similar to what you do with celery). This is achieved by drawing soil up around the stem to exclude light. Be careful not to draw soil over the top of the leek (where the leaves turn in to stem) - you will end up with soil down the inside of the leek which will be a nightmare to remove when cooking. A cleaner method than using soil, is to pop the insert from a kitchen roll around the leek. This works well.

Deep-fried Courgette Flowers stuffed with Goats Cheese and Lavender Honey

DONAL SKEHAN

One of my favorite dishes at the *Salt Yard* restaurant in London is these deep-fried courgette flowers. The vibrant courgette flowers are stuffed with a bright and grassy, creamy goats cheese and then deep fried in a light and crisp tempura style batter and finally drizzled with a sweet lavender honey. Recreating them at home is easier than I had originally thought and if you spot some in the market, snap them up, they make a superb summer starter. The male flowers don't have the small courgettes attached so make sure you choose the female variety with immature fruit attached.

SERVES 2-4

8-12 baby courgettes with the flower attached

250g of soft goats cheese

2 sprigs of thyme, leaves finely chopped

2-3 tablespoons of lavender honey

1 litre of sunflower oil to fry

FOR THE BATTER:

8 tablespoons of plain flour

8 tablespoons of ice cold sparkling water

sea salt and ground black pepper

From Donal Skehan www.donalskehan.com

In a bowl mix together the goats cheese and thyme leaves. Open each courgette flower and carefully stuff with a heaped teaspoon of goats cheese. Seal the flowers by gently twisting the tops of the petals around the goats cheese.

Heat the oil in a large high sided pot over a medium heat. Mix together the flour and sparkling water until you have a light and runny batter (it should be just thick enough to be able to coat the courgette flowers) and season with sea salt and ground black pepper.

Carefully working beside the hot oil, dip the courgette flowers into the batter to coat completely, allowing any excess to drip off. Gently place the coated courgettes, in batches of 4 at a time, into the hot oil and allow to cook until golden for 3-4 minutes, turning halfway through the cooking time if necessary. You can check if they are tender by piercing the flesh with a fork.

Using a slotted spoon, place the cooked courgette flowers on a plate lined with kitchen paper.

Serve the crispy courgette flowers immediately drizzled with lavender honey and seasoned with sea salt and ground black pepper.

Chard and New Potato Curry

HUGH FEARNLEY-WHITTINGSTALL

This hearty curry is fantastic in late summer or early autumn. If you want to make it ahead of time and refrigerate or freeze it, leave out the yoghurt and add it at the last minute, just before serving.

SERVES 4

about 500g Swiss chard

2 tablespoons sunflower oil

1 onion, halved and finely sliced

3 garlic cloves, peeled

1 green chilli, deseeded and finely chopped

3cm piece of ginger, peeled and chopped

1 teaspoon garam masala

½ teaspoon mustard seeds

½ teaspoon ground cumin

¼ teaspoon ground turmeric

3 cardamom pods, bashed

350g new potatoes, quartered

250g plain (full-fat) yoghurt

1½ tablespoons tomato purée

a small bunch of coriander, roughly chopped

a small handful of almonds, cashews or pistachios, toasted and chopped

sea salt and freshly ground black pepper

From *River Cottage Veg Every Day* by Hugh Fearnley-Whittingstall. Published by Bloomsbury 2011.

Separate the chard leaves from the stalks. Cut the stalks into 2–3cm pieces and roughly chop the leaves.

Heat the oil in a large saucepan over a medium heat, add the onion and fry until just golden.

Meanwhile, pound the garlic, chilli and ginger together with a pinch of salt to a paste. Add to the onion and cook, stirring, for a couple of minutes. Tip in the rest of the spices and stir for a minute or two.

Add the potatoes and chopped chard stalks and fry, stirring frequently, for 5 minutes, so that they are well coated with the spice mixture. Pour in about 400ml water – enough to just cover the veg.

Bring to a simmer, cover and cook for 10–12 minutes until the potatoes are just tender. Add the chard leaves, stir and cook until just wilted. In a bowl, whisk together the yoghurt, tomato purée and some of the hot liquid from the curry. Remove the curry from the heat, stir in the yoghurt mixture, return to the heat and warm through very gently (if it gets too hot, the yoghurt will curdle). Stir in most of the coriander.

Taste and add salt and pepper if needed. Scatter over the toasted nuts and remaining coriander, then serve with rice and naan or chapattis.

VARIATIONS

Spinach and new potato curry; Use 600–700g spinach in place of the chard. Remove any tough stalks and add the leaves to the curry once the potatoes are done. Cook for a minute or two before adding the yoghurt mixture.

Winter kale and potato curry; Use maincrop potatoes, peeled and cut into bite-sized chunks, rather than new potatoes, and replace the chard with kale. Discard the kale stalks, roughly shred the leaves, and add them when the potatoes are nearly done. Simmer for 2–3 minutes, or until tender.

Courgette Linguine with Confit Tomato

DYLAN MCGRATH

SERVES 4

400g blanched linguine

2 yellow courgettes

1 sprig of thyme

25ml olive oil

salt

black pepper

LINGUINE SAUCE

200ml crème fraîche

100ml veg stock

1 teaspoon baby capers

1 teaspoon caper paste

pinch salt

pinch sugar

half a lemon

finely chopped chives

CONFIT TOMATO

3 plum tomatoes

1 clove garlic, finely sliced

4 small sprigs thyme

1 tablespoon olive oil

fresh basil leaves

cherry vine tomato

From Dylan McGrath
www.dylanmcgrath.com

To prepare the courgettes

Cut the courgette in half length ways and scoop out the seeds with a tea spoon leaving it looking like a canoe. Rub in olive oil and season with salt and freshly ground black pepper. Then heat a pan. Add a little olive oil, thyme and roast on both sides on a medium heat for about 5 minutes until courgette is cooked but still a little firm.

To make the linguine sauce

Add the crème fraîche, veg stock and caper paste to a small sauce pan, bring to the boil and reduce slowly until the sauce thickens slightly. Then add the capers, sugar and salt. Then add your blanched linguini, chives and lemon and coat in the sauce.

To make the confit tomato

Quarter the tomatoes and remove the seeds. Roll in olive oil, salt and a little icing sugar. Place on a baking tray. Add the thyme and sliced garlic onto each quarter. Then place the tray in a pre-heated oven at 160˚C for 20 minutes.

To serve

Take the roasted courgette, then take the pasta rolled in the sauce and fill it in to the courgette. Add the confit tomato, some torn fresh basil and sliced cherry vine tomato. Finish with some freshly shaved Parmesan.

Asian Greens, Egg Pancake and Rice Noodle Salad

JOY LARKCOM

You can use any combination or quantity of greens for this salad, but the herbs are vital for its fresh, vibrant character. The dressing uses commercial chilli sauce. Use your favourite brand or, if you don't have one, add a finely chopped fresh red chilli and a little more sugar.

SERVES 2

2 large eggs

200g/7oz rice vermicelli noodles

2 handfuls of a mixture of mizuna, mibuna and baby mustard leaves

1 small head pak choi, sliced

2 spring onions, sliced

15-20cm/6-8in cucumber, cut in thin sticks

small handful of bean sprouts

2 tablespoons mint leaves, chopped

2 tablespoons coriander leaves

2 tablespoons cashews, lightly toasted

FOR THE DRESSING

3 tablespoons lemon or lime juice

1 tablespoon sugar

1 tablespoon soy sauce

1 tablespoon chilli sauce

1 teaspoon toasted sesame oil

1 teaspoon grated fresh ginger

Beat the eggs lightly and season with salt and pepper. In a heavy frying pan, make one or two pancakes with the eggs, depending on the size of your pan, cooking them on both sides over medium heat until cooked through but not coloured. Slice the cooked pancakes into strips 1cm (½in) wide.

Break up the rice noodles if they are very long. Drop into boiling water and simmer gently until cooked. Drain and cool. Combine all the salad ingredients in a bowl and gently mix in the eggroll slices and noodles. Mix together the dressing ingredients and pour over the salad. Toss gently and serve in deep bowls.

From *Oriental Vegetables* by Joy Larkcom.
Published by Frances Lincoln 2007.

SERVES 4, OR 6 TO 8
AS A SIDE DISH

1 tablespoon cumin seeds

5 cups sliced carrots

½ medium white onion,
minced

2 cups chickpeas, drained
and rinsed if using canned

2 tablespoons olive oil

½ teaspoon sea salt

¼ teaspoon black pepper

½ cup vegetable broth

2 tablespoons lemon juice

2 cups cooked wild rice or
wild rice blend

¼ cup pepitas

1 ounce feta cheese

Jess Murphy is Head Chef at Kai
in Galway.

Cumin-Roasted Carrots with Wild Rice and Chickpeas

JESS MURPHY

This recipe takes fresh summer carrots and turns them in to a delicious meal or supper. Carrots and cumin are a brilliant combination and the rice makes it filling too.

Preheat oven to 190°C. In a small skillet, heat the cumin seeds over medium heat until fragrant, 2 to 3 minutes. Place in a spice grinder or use a mortar to grind the cumin seeds into a powder. (You should have 1 scant tablespoon of ground cumin.)

In a roasting pan, combine the sliced carrots, minced onion, chickpeas, olive oil, and cumin powder. Stir to coat carrots with cumin and oil. Pour the vegetable broth and lemon juice into pan and cover with tin foil. Roast carrots for 30 minutes until tender, remove foil, and cook for another 10 to 15 minutes until carrots are tender.

Remove carrots from oven and toss with wild rice, pepitas, and feta cheese. Serve warm.

Carrot Top Pesto

JESS MURPHY

MAKES ABOUT 1 CUP

2 cups of carrot tops

2 tbsp vegetable oil

Kosher salt

freshly ground pepper

1 garlic clove

3 tbsp macadamia nuts or pine nuts

½ cup fresh basil leaves

¼ cup finely grated Parmesan

½ cup extra-virgin olive oil

Jess Murphy is Head Chef at Kai in Galway.

We're all guilty of ditching the carrot tops, but they can be a nutritious, seasonal ingredient in their own right.

Pulse garlic and nuts in a food processor until a coarse paste forms. Add the basil, Parmesan, and carrot tops; process again until a coarse paste forms. With the motor running, stream in the olive oil: ¼ cup will make a thicker pesto that's good for spreading on crostini and sandwiches, while ½ cup will make a thinner pesto that's good for tossing with pasta. Stop and scrape down the sides of the bowl as needed and blend until the mixture is a uniform paste.

Taste the pesto and blend in more salt, garlic, nuts, or cheese as needed.

Baked Raspberry and Ricotta Cheesecake

RACHEL ALLEN

In this variation on the classic American dessert, ricotta is used rather than cream cheese for a lighter texture, while the raspberries add a tangy, refreshing touch.

SERVES 8-10

50g (2oz) butter, melted, plus extra for greasing

150g (5oz) (about 12) digestive biscuits

1 x 500g tub of ricotta cheese

200g (7oz) crème fraîche

3 eggs

175g (6oz) caster sugar

1 tbsp runny honey

grated zest of 1 lemon

2 tsp vanilla extract

275g (10oz) fresh raspberries

icing sugar, for dusting

20cm (8in) diameter spring-form/loose-bottomed cake tin

From *Home Cooking* by Rachel Allen. Published by Collins, 2009.

Preheat the oven to 180° C (350°F), Gas mark 4. Grease the sides and base of the cake tin.

Place the biscuits in a food processor and blend until quite fine. Alternatively place them in a plastic bag and bash with a rolling pin. Mix the crushed biscuits with the melted butter and tip into the prepared tin. Press down into the base of the tin to form an even layer.

Wash the processor bowl and blade, reset and add the ricotta, crème fraiche, eggs, sugar, honey, lemon zest and vanilla extract. Blend for a few seconds until smooth and well combined. Alternatively, place all the ingredients in a large bowl and blend using a hand-held electric beater. Crush 100g (3 ½ oz) of the raspberries with a fork and stir them into the mixture.

Pour the mixture onto the biscuit base in the tin and gently shake and tilt the tin so that the ricotta mixture forms a level layer (minding the loose bottom of the tin!). Bake in the oven for 40-45 minutes or until the cheesecake is pale golden and wobbles slightly in the middle when you shake the tin. Remove, cover with foil and leave in a warm place to completely cool before storing in the fridge over night. Don't worry if the top has cracked when you take it out again as the remaining raspberries will cover this.

Run a knife around the edge to loosen the cheesecake and remove it from the tin. Transfer to a serving plate and scatter the remaining raspberries on top. Dust with icing sugar and serve.

West Cork Cream Pudding

with Meath Strawberries and fresh Yoghurt Mousse, Soda Bread Sugar Biscuits and Irish Apple Balsamic Vinegar Meringues

ROSS LEWIS

We created this dish for the state visit at Dublin castle, hosted by President McAleese to honour the visit of Queen Elizabeth II to the Irish Republic. As it was the first ever visit by a reigning British monarch, we wanted the dish to entertain the diners visually as much as it would on the palate. The presentation looks like the setting for an Irish fairytale and the flavours evoke childhood memories, yet they are matched by sophisticated textures and flavours. What a dainty dish to set before a queen.

SERVES 8

FOR THE SODA BREAD SUGAR BISCUITS

100g butter

300g dark muscovado sugar

100g plain flour

160g egg whites

Brown soda bread powder for sprinkling

FOR THE CREAM PUDDING

700ml milk

300ml Glenilen cream

100g sugar

5 vanilla pods

15g gold leaf gelatine

FOR THE STRAWBERRY CONSOMMÉ

300g strawberries

50g of sugar (1st)

Juice of 1 lime

20g of sugar

2g of gold leaf gelatine

Soda bread sugar biscuits

Melt the butter in a pan and add the sugar, stirring to dissolve. Remove from the heat and tip in the flour and egg whites, then whisk until smooth. Pass through a sieve and chill for 24 hours. The next day, preheat the oven to 170°C. Spread the tuile mix on a lined baking tray lined with a silpat. Using a 4 x 2 cm template, make 8 tuiles and sprinkle with an even layer of the brown soda bread powder. Bake for 9 minutes until they have turned a rich brown colour. Leave for a minute to set and then transfer to a rack to cool completely.

Cream pudding

Bring the milk and cream to the boil. Add the sugar and vanilla pods, and leave to infuse for 30 minutes, Soak the gelatine in cold water for 10 minutes, then squeeze out the excess liquid. Return the milk and cream mix to the heat, and bring to a simmer. Whisk in the soaked gelatine until dissolved, then strain through a fine chinois. Chill for 3-4 hours. Line the base of a 10 x 3cm ring mould with cling film and fill to just over half way up the sides. Chill for at least another hour.

Strawberry consommé

Place all the ingredients in a bowl, except the second amount of sugar and the gelatine, and cook in a bain-marie set over a pan of simmering water for 3 hours. Strain through a fine chinois and chill for at least an hour. Take 130ml of the strawberry consommé, add the second amount of sugar and bring to the boil. Meanwhile, soak the gelatine in water for 10 minutes, then squeeze out the excess liquid and whisk into the strawberry juice until dissolved. Leave to cool, then pour a thin layer of jelly over the top of each set cream pudding and chill for one hour. Reserve 200ml of the consommé to make the strawberry cream for serving.

FOR THE APPLE BALSAMIC VINEGAR MERINGUES

100g egg whites

100g caster sugar

Pinch of crème tar tar

120g icing sugar, sieved

50ml apple balsamic cider vinegar

5g hy-foamer

FOR THE YOGHURT AND VANILLA MOUSSE

1g gold leaf gelatine

85ml Glenilen cream

65g sugar

2 vanilla pods, split in half and seeds scraped out

350g Compsey Creamery Greek-style yoghurt

TO SERVE

75ml Glenilen cream

4 fresh strawberries, cut into slices, ends discarded

24 dried strawberry pieces

10ml raspberry vinegar

From Chapter One: A Story of Irish Food by Ross Lewis. Published by Gill & Macmillan, 2013.

Apple balsamic vinegar meringues

Preheat the oven to 70°C. Whisk the egg whites in a Kitchen Aid with the whisk attachment on a slow speed until frothy. Pour in the sugar, add the crème of tar tar and hy-foamer, and continue to whisk until glossy and stiff. Add the sieved icing sugar and balsamic vinegar, and whisk for 1 minute. Put into a piping bag with a No.1 nozzle and pipe 8 meringues onto a baking tray lined with silicone paper then cook for 3 hours.

Yoghurt and vanilla mousse

Soak the gelatine in cold water for 10 minutes, then squeeze out the excess liquid. Meanwhile, bring the cream, sugar and vanilla seeds to the boil. Whisk in the gelatine until dissolved. Remove from the heat and whisk in the yoghurt. Put into a foam gun and charge with 1 gas charger. Chill for at least 2 hours.

Serving

Take the reserved 200ml of strawberry consommé and stir in 75ml of cream. Using a hot knife, unmould the cream puddings onto serving plates and then pour around the strawberry cream to flood each plate. Arrange fresh strawberry slices on each pudding, followed by pieces of dried strawberries and pieces of soda bread sugar biscuit. Add an apple balsamic vinegar meringue to each one and some dots of the raspberry vinegar. Finish with a dome of the yoghurt mousse.

August

IF YOU ALLOW IT TO BE, the harvest can be a time of incredible celebration, and it is quite right that it should be so. We should be celebrating at this time of the year even though it might seem kind of quaint to do so.

The joy of the harvest is something that the food chain's assault on seasonality has deprived us of, for if every vegetable is available all the year round, then of course there is no compelling reason to celebrate the harvest months. As GIYers, we step up to reclaim the joy of the harvest.

After 5-6 months of hard work and preparation, August is a month of 'super-abundance' with fruit trees laden down with fruit and the veggie patch heaving with produce. That generally means we need to get stuck in and roll up our sleeves – doing whatever it takes to use the fruits of our labour: lifting crops and getting them in to storage, and shelling, dicing, chopping and pickling in preparation for the winter months ahead.

Don't forget to take time to enjoy the fruits of your labour and have heroic meals in convivial company!

THIS MONTH'S TOP JOBS

* Final monthly indoor sowing of lettuce, oriental greens, annual spinach, calabrese and coriander.

* For winter salad leaves in the polytunnel or greenhouse, sow now in module trays: chervil, lamb's lettuce, chard, winter purslane, salad onions and oriental greens.

* Remember the lean months – store, freeze, pickle and make jams, chutneys etc.

* Sow green manures to improve soil fertility.

* Mulch plants to retain moisture.

Things to Do in... *August*

PREPARATION

Green manures are plants which are grown specifically to improve soil fertility and useful at times when beds are empty. Grow directly in the bed and then cut down and dig in to the soil, improving the soil structure and nutrient level as well as preventing the leaching of nutrients. Green manures include mustard, buckwheat, radish, rye, alfalfa, clover and vetches.

TO DO LIST

Give pumpkins plenty of water and apply a high-potash liquid feed. Nip out the growing points to encourage the fruits to swell. Put something under fruits if they are resting on soil to prevent the underside from rotting. Cut back any herbs that have finished flowering to encourage fresh growth. Continued vigilance is required with your brassicas. Netting the plants is the most effective way of keeping butterflies away. Lift the netting regularly and remove eggs and caterpillars from leaves. Keep weeding – in particular, don't allow weeds to go to seed as they will produce lots and lots of other weeds!! Keep watering - mulch around plants to retain moisture in really hot weather. Keep an eye on your apple and other fruit trees – prune if they have made too much new growth.

SOWING SEEDS AND PLANTING OUT

This is the final monthly indoor sowing of lettuce, oriental greens, annual spinach, calabrese and coriander.
For winter salad leaves in the polytunnel or greenhouse, sow now in module trays: chervil, lamb's lettuce, chard, winter purslane, salad onions and oriental greens. Plant strawberries now for a good crop next June. Propagate rosemary, sage and mint from cuttings now.

HARVESTING – WHAT'S IN SEASON?

August is truly a month of plenty in the garden so enjoy! As vegetables and soft fruits continue, they are joined at the end of this month by tree fruits like apple and plum. Pick beetroot regularly as they reach the size you require – if left to grow too large they will lose their tenderness. Each sweet corn plant will produce two beautiful yellow cobs. Pick them as soon as the 'tassels' wither to brown and when a creamy

Right: *Some of my favourite tom varieties – including the delectable sungold.*

liquid squirts out of the grains when you squeeze. Cook immediately. Continue to harvest beetroot, tomatoes, carrots, cabbage, cauliflower, peas, broad beans, French and runner beans, salad leaves, radish, turnip, potato, onions, peppers and chilli-peppers, aubergine, globe artichoke, courgettes, cucumber, gooseberries, raspberries and currants. With the abundance of fresh produce, consider storing some for winter use, e.g. freeze, make pickles and chutneys from onions, cauliflower, green beans, tomatoes, cucumber, apples, plums. Make special vinegars from excess herbs, onions, chilli-peppers and garlic. Make jams, curds and jellies from strawberries, raspberries, blackberries, blueberries, gooseberries, currants (red/white/black), beetroot and mint.

Veg of the Month - Tomatoes

WHY GROW THEM?

Few vegetables have suffered at the hands of the commercial food chain as much as the tomato. The simple fact of the matter is that most of the tomatoes that we buy year in, year out in our supermarkets taste of absolutely nothing at all. It is often not until you grow your own that you realise this! The home-grown tomato, on the other hand, is a delectable treat, best eaten fresh in the warmth of the greenhouse for maximum effect. Sure, tomatoes need a good deal of TLC – pinching out side shoots, watering, feeding etc. But it's worth the effort for the sheer diversity of sizes, shapes, colours and flavours that you can grow yourself.

SOWING

There are basically two types of tomato plants. Vine (or cordon) tomato plants are an orderly affair and have a tall central stem. Bush tomatoes are more compact but disorderly – they have trailing side branches. Being an insanely neat kind of a person, I generally only grow the vine varieties.
Tomatoes have a long growing season and can be started in February indoors on a heating mat to get a head start. Otherwise wait until March. Sow seeds in pots or module trays indoors in a warm, sunny spot. When they have developed three true leaves prick out in to 3-inch pots. They won't be going in to the soil until May. Keep the potting compost moist.

GROWING

Though lots of GIYers have grown tomatoes successfully outdoors, to my mind this Mediterranean vegetable fares best in the warmth of a greenhouse, polytunnel or conservatory. They can be sown direct in the soil but will also grow well in pots as long as the container is good and deep (toms are quite deep rooting, and hungry). Grow bags also work well. Wherever you plant them, make sure it's the warmest, sunniest place possible. They like rich, fertile soil – dig in a well-rotted manure or compost before planting or use poultry manure pellets.
Vine tomatoes grow very tall and will require support – an ideal way to provide this is to put strong twine around the roots of the plant before you plant it in to the soil. This twine is then buried in the soil and tied to a horizontal on the roof of the greenhouse or tunnel, providing a taut vertical for the main stem to grow up. Leave 40-50cm between plants.

Vine varieties of toms produce two types of side stems: (1) 'trusses' or fruit bearing branches on which the tomatoes grow and (2) leaf stems. As the plant grows, 'side shoots' regularly appear in the angle between the main stem and leaf stems. These waste the plants energy if you allow them to grow and therefore need to be regularly 'pinched out'. When the plants are 4ft tall remove the leave stalks below the first fruit truss. This will improve air circulation around the base of the plants and makes it easier to water. Remove yellowing leaves as they appear.

Water evenly and regularly - irregular watering causes fruit to split. Never water the foliage on a tom plant as it will burn in the sunlight. Approximate water requirements are 11 litres per plant per week.

Left to its own devices, the main stem of a healthy tom plant will just keep on growing up and up. But growing toms is a balancing act between allowing the plant to grow to a good height and forcing it to focus on producing fruit. Keep an eye on the number of trusses that are forming on the plant. If the plant is healthy allow seven or eight trusses to form. If it is not healthy, stop when the plant has formed five or six trusses by pinching out the growing point (top of the main stem).

Once toms are starting to appear, feed fortnightly with a high-potash feed. Organic liquid tom feeds are available commercially or you can make your own comfrey tea by soaking 500g of comfrey leaves in 3 gallons of water and leave to stew for a month. Dilute before applying to plants - one part comfrey tea to ten parts water.

HARVESTING

Harvest when the fruits are ripe. Fruit will split if left on the plants so remove as it ripens – surplus fruit can be made in to sauces for the freezer. Plants sown later may continue to produce fruit right in to late October and early November. You are likely to be left with lots of green fruit at the end of the season – use these for chutneys. Never serve tomatoes straight

from the fridge – flavour is best when served warm.

GIY RECOMMENDED VARIETIES

Sungold, Tigerella, Gardeners Delight, San Marzano, Beefsteak, Roma.

PROBLEMS

The best way to avoid problems is to ensure that air is circulating around the plants. The same blight that affects potatoes can be devastating to tomatoes, particularly outdoor ones (though it can make its way in to greenhouses and polytunnels too). It causes leaves to curl and blacken. Try removing affected leaves or plants quickly but there's little you can do once it takes hold. The most common pests are whitefly, aphids and spider mites – sowing marigolds around your tom plants will help. Rolling or curling of tomato leaves is common and can be due to wide variation between day and night time temperatures. It is not a problem.

GIY TIPS

■ For effective watering sink a pot in the ground beside the plant and water in to this. This gets water right down to the roots.
■ At the end of the season put a layer of green tomatoes in a drawer with a ripe apple or banana. These ripening fruits give off the ripening gas ethylene which encourages the tomatoes to ripen.
■ Bake surplus tomatoes in the oven for 8 hours on a very low heat – cut them in half first and drizzle with some oil and salt. These "sundried" tomatoes can be stored in olive oil or frozen.

MONTHLY INSIGHT– SAVING SEEDS

Man has been cultivating food for about 10,000 years. For the vast majority of that time, seed varieties were kept alive by being passed on from generation to generation. It's only really in the last 100 years that seed ownership has effectively passed in to the hands of corporations – in that time in Ireland over 90% of seed varieties have disappeared. This is grim news because of course it means that the very things that give us such immense joy in our GIYing – the abundant diversity of shapes, sizes, colours and flavours - are being lost in the interest of yields and profits.

Protecting our food heritage is as important as protecting our cultural heritage, and our native seed varieties are just as important as our native songs, poetry, art and historical artefacts. By saving your own seed (particularly if they are of traditional, local varieties) you are playing a small part in keeping that food heritage alive. Seed saving is also an important educational tool - whenever I do it, I am always struck by how much the process can teach us (in a typically natural and practical way) about the cycle of growth, maturity, decay and regrowth that's so essential to life on this planet.

HOW TO SAVE YOUR OWN TOMATO SEEDS

If you had a variety of tomato that was a particular success this year, why not try saving the seeds to grow next year's plants? You should only save seed from open-pollinated varieties of tomatoes, and not hybrids (if in doubt check the seed packet). Pick a nice big, ripe tomato and cut it in half. Squeeze the contents (seeds, gel and juice - not flesh) in to a cup or container and label the cup with the variety. Half fill the cup with water. After a few days a mould will form on the water, which is a sign that the seed coating has dissolved.

Pour off the water and any floating seeds (these are duds that won't germinate). The good seeds should be on the bottom of the cup. Rinse the seeds under a cold tap in a very fine mesh strainer. Put the seeds in a single layer on a paper plate and leave for a few days to dry. Bag them up in a labelled envelope and store them somewhere cool (or refrigerate) until next spring.

AUGUST TIPS

SOW TURNIPS

Turnips are very easy to grow and because they produce a crop so quickly, they are an ideal candidate for a late-summer sowing. You can even slot them in to a bed that has been freed up by harvesting another vegetable (I generally sow them in the onion bed). Note that we are talking about turnips here (with the white flesh) as opposed to swedes (yellow flesh) which take much longer to mature - it's too late now to sow swedes this year. If you sow turnips now, they will be ready to eat in 6-8 weeks (end September). Harvest when relatively small if possible and don't leave them in the ground too late in the winter - they will be a target for mice and slugs. Water well in dry spells to prevent cracking.

NEWSPAPER AND GRASS COMPOST

Here's how to make great compost for your veggie patch using two of the great waste-creators in the home and garden - newspapers and grass cuttings. Build a heap (the ground surface area should be 1m by 1m) of alternating 30cm layers of crumpled newspaper and grass cuttings. Allow the heap to get quite tall - 4-6ft - and then leave it to rot down for a year.

HARVEST ONIONS

Onions are ready to harvest when the foliage turns yellow and topples over (approximately 20 weeks after sowing). Gently loosen the soil around the onions at this point (or turn the onion very carefully and very slightly in the soil) and leave for another two weeks. Loosening the soil like this allows the onion to expand in the soil. Then lift carefully (you may be able to ease them out without using a fork, but be careful not to damage the necks as you pull them). For storage, leave to dry on a rack in the sun (or indoors in a shed/greenhouse/polytunnel if weather is wet) for about 10 days. Then plait them in ropes or hang in nets. Make sure to store them somewhere very dry - if there is any moisture at all in the air, the onions may rot. Check the rope frequently and use/remove any onions that are showing any signs of softening. Tip: if you can requisition an old pair of tights, each leg will make a great net for hanging onions!

HOME-MADE MILDEW REMEDY

To get on top of mildew on plants (a particular issue in a damp summer), try this home-made remedy. Mix half a tablespoon of bicarbonate of soda with a pint of soapy water in a spray bottle. Add a drop of vegetable oil (which will help it to stick to dry leaves). Spray both sides of leaves of vulnerable plants (e.g. dill, parsley, parsnips, peas, beans, carrots, turnips, cabbage, broccoli, cauliflower, radishes, beets, etc.).

Onion braid on it's way to the kitchen.

Tomato Fennel Soup
(Zuppa di Pomodoro e Finocchio)

CATHERINE FULVIO

Having the chopped fennel in this soup means there is no need for extra herbs or anything else. This is a lovely classic southern Italian combination and the beauty of the dish is it's simple, earthy flavours. In the summer, we make courgette and fennel soup at Ballyknocken, as we seem to have an endless supply of courgettes. I think it has something to do with the ample quantities of rain mixed with the sunshine!

SERVES 4

2 tbsp extra virgin olive oil

2 fennel bulbs, diced

1 red pepper, diced

2 garlic cloves, thinly sliced

400g fresh or tinned tomatoes, chopped

800ml chicken stock

2 tbsp tomato purée

salt and freshly ground black pepper

From *Eat like an Italian* by Catherine Fulvio. Gill and Macmillan 2012.

Heat the olive oil in a large saucepan. Add the fennel and red pepper and sauté on a low heat until softened. Add the garlic and cook for 1 minute more.

Add the tomatoes, stock and tomato purée and simmer for 20-25 minutes.

Pour into a food processor and blend until smooth. Return to the pan and heat through.

Season to taste and serve.

Sundried Tomato Pesto

NEVEN MAGUIRE

MAKES ABOUT 400ML (14FL OZ)

175g (6oz) semi sun-dried tomatoes, roughly chopped

8 large fresh basil leaves

2 garlic cloves, peeled

200ml (7fl oz) olive or rapeseed oil

sea salt and freshly ground black pepper

From *The MacNean Restaurant Cookbook* by Neven Maguire. Gill and Macmillan, 2012.

Place the semi sun-dried tomatoes in a food processor or blender with the basil leaves and garlic and pulse to finely chop. Switch the machine back on and slowly pour in the oil through the feeder tube until the pesto has emulsified. Transfer to a bowl with a spatula and season to taste.

PREPARE AHEAD: This can be made up to 3–4 days in advance and kept covered with clingfilm in the fridge.

Tomato Fondue

DARINA ALLEN

Tomato fondue has a number of uses. We serve it as a vegetable, a sauce for pasta, filling for omelettes and topping for pizza. It is vital for the success of this dish that the onions are completely soft before the tomatoes are added. In the winter, you can use tinned or frozen tomatoes but they need to be cooked for longer.

SERVES ABOUT 6

1 tablespoon extra virgin olive oil

110g (4oz) onions, sliced

1 garlic clove, crushed

900g (2lb) very ripe tomatoes, peeled

salt, freshly ground pepper and sugar to taste

2 tablespoons of any or a combination of the following: freshly chopped mint, thyme, parsley, lemon balm, marjoram or torn basil

A few drops of balsamic vinegar (optional)

From *Forgotten Skills of Cooking* by Darina Allen. Kyle Cathie Limited, 2009.

Heat the oil in a casserole or stainless-steel saucepan. Add the onions and garlic and toss until coated. Cover and sweat on a gentle heat until the onions and garlic are soft but not coloured. Slice the tomatoes and add with all the juice to the onions. Season with salt, freshly ground pepper and sugar. Add a generous sprinkling of herbs.

Cook, uncovered, for about 10 minutes, or until the tomatoes soften.

A few drops of balsamic vinegar added at the end of cooking greatly enhance the flavour.

Channelled Wrack and Ginger Miso Slaw

SALLY MCKENNA

SERVES 6-8

1 head red cabbage, shredded

2 carrots, peeled and cut into thin strips

¼ red onion, peeled and grated

salt and pepper

handful channelled wrack

tablespoon sesame seeds

DRESSING

¼ cup white miso

3 tablespoons rice syrup (or honey)

¼ cup mirin

3 tablespoons sesame oil

juice of half a lemon

knob of grated ginger

From *Extreme Greens: Understanding Seaweeds* by Sally McKenna. Published by Estragon Press 2013.

Mix together the cabbage, carrot and onion in a large bowl. Season. Toss well to evenly distribute the onion.

Blend the dressing ingredients together until smooth. Season the dressing to taste with salt and pepper.

Put a saucepan of water on to boil and simmer the channelled wrack for approximately five minutes. Chop the seaweed into bite-size lengths.

Toss the cabbage mixture in approximately half of the dressing (save the remainder in the fridge for another salad).

Stir in the seaweed, and scatter over the sesame seeds.

Sally and John McKenna of John and Sally McKennas' Guides. www.guides.ie

 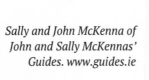

Wexford Strawberry and Apple Crumble

KEVIN DUNDON

Replace the apples with rhubarb or blackberries if you'd prefer. The crumble mixture works really well on top of any fruit and the dark muscovado gives it that classic crunchiness.

SERVES 6

300g sugar pastry

1 egg yolk beaten with 2 tbsp water

225g apples, peeled, cored and cut into slices (such as Granny Smith or Coxes)

225g strawberries, hulled and halved if large

40g caster sugar

finely grated rind and juice of 1 small orange

25g plain flour

25g wholemeal flour

¼ tsp baking powder

25g dark muscovado sugar

25g blanched almonds, finely chopped

1 tsp fine oatmeal

25g butter, cut into cubes

crème fraîche, to serve

From *Full on Irish - Creative Contemporary Cooking* by Kevin Dundon. Epicure Press, 2007.

Divide the sugar pastry into six pieces and use to line 6 x 10 cm/4 in individual tartlet tins that are 4 cm/1 ½in deep. As this pastry is so short you may find it easier to press it into the tins in an even layer using the tips of your fingers. Arrange on a large baking sheet and chill for at least 15 minutes to allow the pastry to rest.

Preheat the oven to 180°C/350°F/Gas 4. Line each pastry case with a circle of non-stick parchment paper that is first crumpled up to make it easier to handle. Fill with baking beans or dried pulses and bake for about 15 minutes until the pastry cases look 'set', but not coloured.

Carefully remove the paper from the pastry cases, then brush the insides with the egg wash to form a seal. Place in the oven for another 5 minutes or until the bases are firm to the touch and the sides are lightly coloured. Remove from the oven and leave until cool enough to handle, then carefully take out of the tins and leave to cool completely on a wire rack.

Reduce the oven temperature to 160°C/325°F/Gas 3. Place the apples and strawberries in a pan with the caster sugar, orange rind and juice. Bring to a simmer, then cover and cook gently for 5 minutes until the fruits are tender but still holding their shape. Remove from the heat and leave to cool.

Sift the plain and wholemeal flour into a bowl with the baking powder, then tip the residue from the sieve back into the bowl. Stir in the muscovado sugar, almonds and oatmeal. Rub in the butter until the mixture resembles breadcrumbs. Divide the cooled fruit mixture among the pastry cases and sprinkle the crumble on top. Arrange on a large baking sheet and bake for another 20-25 minutes until the crumble topping is crisp and golden brown.

To serve, arrange the crumbles on serving plates warm or cold and using two dessertspoons dipped in hot water add a quenelle of crème fraîche to each one.

Tarte aux Framboises

A little effort is required here to achieve pâtisserie-level presentation. It's amazing what some clever placing of raspberries and a light dusting of icing sugar will do, though, if your pastry base is less than neat. Taste-wise, there can be no short cuts with the shortcrust, I'm afraid. It's homemade or not at all! In fact, along with the flavour of fresh raspberries, it's really what this dessert is all about, the crumbling, buttery, sweet shortcrust acting as a canvas for tart fruit smoothed through the palate by rich vanilla crème pâtissière.

SERVES 6-8

500g fresh raspberries

icing sugar (optional) for serving

FOR THE SWEET SHORTCRUST PASTRY

250g plain flour

2 teaspoons sugar or, much better, vanilla sugar

A pinch of fleur de sel

125g very cold unsalted butter, cut into small cubes

FOR THE CRÈME PÂTISSIÈRE

400ml whole milk

1 vanilla pod, split in half

5 large egg yolks

100g sugar

50g plain flour, sifted

From *Trish's French Kitchen* by Trish Deseine. Kyle Cathie 2008.

To make the sweet shortcrust pastry, sift the flour into a bowl, add the sugar and salt and mix. Drop in the butter and work it into the flour with the tips of your fingers. Lift up the mixture as much as possible, so that air gets in, to make the pastry crumbly and light.

When the mixture resembles fine breadcrumbs, make a well in the centre and pour in a couple of table-spoonfuls of very cold water. Mix it in quickly, kneading with your fingers and then your hands to make a ball of pastry. Cover the ball with cling film and chill in the freezer for 30 minutes or in the fridge for an hour or so.

Remove the pastry and roll it out into a circle large enough to line a 20 or 22cm non-stick tart base (there will be a little left over). Put the base in the fridge for 30 minutes or in the freezer for 15 minutes.

Heat the oven to 200°C/400°F/gas mark 6. Prick the base of the tart with a fork to stop it puffing up, then line with baking parchment. Fill it with baking beans and cook for 15 minutes or so, until the edges of the pastry are golden. Remove the baking beans. At this stage you could put it back in the oven for 5 minutes or so if you feel the middle has not cooked sufficiently, but it's usually fine. Let the base cool right down.

Meanwhile, make the crème pâtissière by heating the milk in a saucepan with the halved vanilla pod. Bring to the boil but don't let it boil over. As the milk is heating, whisk the egg yolks with the sugar until they are pale and creamy and have doubled in volume. Add the flour and mix well.

Pour the hot milk on to the egg yolks, whisking well. Pour the custard back into the saucepan and slowly heat it again, whisking all the time to get rid of any little lumps of flour, until it thickens. Keep whisking for about 2 minutes – it will be cooked when it turns slightly liquid again (if it isn't cooked, you will taste the flour rather than the eggs and vanilla). Take it off the heat, pour into a bowl and let it cool completely.

Spoon the cooled crème pâtissière into the tart base and smooth it out evenly. Set the raspberries neatly and tightly packed on to it discarding any whose juice leaks out. Dredge with icing sugar just before serving, if you like.

Teeny White Chocolate, Pistachio & Raspberry Tarts

SHARON HEARNE SMITH

These go down a treat at any party, whether the room is full of kids or grown-ups. They're perfect for afternoon tea or make a welcome addition to a picnic hamper or lunchbox. They're also gorgeous as a gift. The cases can be prepared and filled ahead of time, leaving you just the final flourishes to add at the last minute.

MAKES 12

75g unsalted butter

100g digestive biscuits

3tbsp shelled green pistachios

100g white chocolate

50ml double cream

Seeds scraped from 1 vanilla pod

12 fresh raspberries

ESSENTIAL KIT

12-hole mini muffin tin

12 mini paper muffin cases

From *No-Bake Baking* by Sharon Hearne Smith. Published by Quercus 2014.

Line the tin with cases, and line a small tray with parchment paper.

Melt the butter in a large saucepan over a low heat. Blitz the biscuits and 2 tablespoons of the pistachios in a food processor, or seal in a food bag and bash with a rolling pin, until you have fine crumbs and finely crushed nuts. Stir into the melted butter to coat well, and divide evenly between the cases. Press the crumbs firmly into the base and up the sides, cover with cling film and chill for about 1 hour, until set firm.

About 15 minutes before the cases are ready, prepare the filling. Snap the chocolate into a medium heatproof bowl and add the cream. Either melt in the microwave in 30-second blasts, stirring between each go, or over a pan of simmering water, shallow enough that the water doesn't touch the bowl. Once melted, stir until smooth and add the vanilla seeds. Leave to cool to body temperature.

Use the tip of a pointed knife to lift the tarts carefully out of the tin. Gently peel the paper cases away and arrange on the tray. Spoon the filling equally between them and chill for 15 minutes or until the filling is set. These can be prepared a day in advance.

When ready to serve, arrange on a pretty tiered cake stand. Sit a raspberry, pointy side up in the centre of each one. Roughly chop the remaining tablespoon of pistachios and scatter over.

For an added twist . . .

• Substitute the white chocolate with milk or dark.

• Top with a cherry or strawberry instead of a raspberry.

September

THERE'S A DEFINITE SENSE of the summer winding down. The kids are back to school, so it's back to frenetic mornings getting everyone out the door and the daily school runs. Chillier, darker evenings are closing in and I am tempted to light the stove at night time. It seems like only yesterday that we were enjoying up to 18 hours of daylight a day. How odd it all seems!

If you find the change in seasons a bit of a downer, thankfully there's still enough happening in the veg patch to remind us that this is autumn, the season of harvest and 'mellow fruitfulness'. In fact, the veg patch harvest is only just beginning, and will be at its peak for the next two to three months.

The wonderful summer crops are now joined in their abundance by their autumn fruit and veg cousins. So on top of the still resplendent courgettes, tomatoes, peas, beans, potatoes, cucumbers, onions, salad crops and the like, we now get to enjoy pears, plums, apples, autumn raspberries, squashes and pumpkins. Reasons to be cheerful indeed!

Left: *Bumper pear harvest from the end of the garden.*

Things to Do in... *September*

PREPARATION

Lift crops which have finished growing and remove weeds from empty ground. Dress "bare" soil with farmyard manure, compost or plant green manures. If your compost heap is ready, empty it out to make way for new material. If not turn it over every few weeks to improve the decomposition rate. If you want to put in new fruit trees/bushes this autumn, this is a good time to start researching and preparing ground for planting in Oct/Nov.

TO DO LIST

Wasps often replace slugs as the key menace at this time of the year, particularly on tree fruit as it ripens. Wasp traps made from jars of sugary water or leftover marmalade/jam jars are effective. Pick up any windfalls or damaged fruit as it attracts wasps. French bean pods are too tough to eat now so you can leave the pods on the plants to save seed for next year. Remove old canes of summer raspberries once they have finished fruiting.

In the polytunnel or greenhouse continue to water regularly but be careful not to over water the foliage of tomato, aubergine, pepper and chilli-pepper plants as it could encourage grey mould. Start removing leaves from your tomato plants which allows air to circulate around the plants and sunshine to fall on the fruit (which helps them to ripen). As the nights cool down, close up earlier to preserve heat.

If it's dry out, continue to water pumpkins and winter squash plants which are still growing until end of month. Give a good soak once a week to celery, celeriac, courgettes, pumpkin, runner bean and leeks.

SOWING SEEDS AND PLANTING OUT

You could try a final sowing of winter 'salad leaves' for the polytunnel – spinach, lettuce, oriental leaves (like mizuna, pak choi, mustard, rocket etc.), coriander, lamb's lettuce, chervil and the like – they will be really worth it in the New Year when there's almost nothing else to eat, so get sowing! Plant out strawberry runners as early as possible this month. Pot up some strong parsley plants in a large pot for winter use. Woody herbs such as sage, rosemary and thyme often root where their stems touch the soil – separate these out and plant to give them time to establish

Above: *Howdy pardner!*
Middle: *Surprisingly decent aubergine crop from a growbag.*
Top: *Another apple fails to make it to the house.*

before growth stops for the winter. Lots of very well prepared GIYers sow overwintering varieties of peas and broad beans at this time of the year – I have to confess that I generally don't, preferring to take a break from sowing between October and January.

HARVESTING – WHAT'S IN SEASON?

Summer vegetables and fruit are joined by those more traditionally associated with autumn/winter, e.g. parsnips, swedes and celeriac. Lift your onions once the foliage withers and dies - leave them to dry out in the sun or in the polytunnel/greenhouse (but eat a few immediately to savour the taste). The great autumn tree fruits - apples, plums, pears – are

Above: Pumpkins 'curing' in the polytunnel.

now ripe. Pears should be picked when ripe and then stored for several weeks before eating. Continue to harvest salad leaves, tomatoes, shallots, potatoes, carrots, turnips, beetroot, cauliflower, cucumbers, peppers and chilli-peppers, French and runner beans, courgettes, spinach, leeks, red cabbage, summer cabbage, aubergine, sweet corn. Go blackberry picking! It's a busy time in the kitchen converting that hard-won harvest in to fuel for the winter - make soups, jams, chutneys, pickles; freeze, dry and store. Every year around April/May time I wish I had made more chutneys the previous autumn, so don't hold back.

Veg of the Month - *Onions*

WHY GROW THEM?

I love onions because they are one of those vegetables that it's possible to become self-sufficient in, even if you don't have a huge amount of space. A decent sized raised bed for example could produce a couple of hundred onions which would be enough for most families for up to a year. They are relatively low maintenance, easy to grow and store well. Above all, there's nothing better than having onions hanging in your shed and knowing you don't have to buy those dry, tasteless, imported supermarket onions this year!

SOWING

You can grow onions from seed, but I always grow from 'sets' (basically baby onions) – they are cheap, reliable and quick growing. Order sets early in the year – the best varieties sell out quickly. Dig in some well-rotted manure or compost the previous winter and apply an organic fertiliser (like chicken manure pellets) before sowing. Don't plant onions in the same place year after year. Include in your crop rotation.

Sow the onion sets 10cm apart in rows 20cm apart in March/April. Hold off if the weather is very cold – onion sets won't do well in cold, damp soil. Push the set in to the soil so that the tip is just about visible above the surface. Firm in well. Frost can "heave" the sets from the soil at night – if this happens push them back in the next day. Birds can also be a pest at this stage. I cover my onion bed with fleece for the first 3-4 weeks after sowing – this keeps the worst of the weather off them and keeps birds away.

GROWING

Onions hate weed competition so keep your onion bed weed free. Hoe carefully around the bulbs every week or so and hand weed if necessary (particularly between April and June when weeds are at their most aggressive). Water if weather is dry or mulch (but remove mulch when bulbs start to form) – but never overwater. An occasional liquid feed will help.

Left: Onions drying in the potting shed before storage.

HARVESTING

Onions are ready to harvest when foliage turns yellow and topples over (around 20 weeks after sowing). Gently loosen the soil around the onions at this point (or turn the onion very carefully and very slightly in the soil) and leave for another two weeks. Then lift carefully. Onions can be eaten fresh from soil. For storage, leave to dry on rack in the sun (or indoors in greenhouse/polytunnel if weather is wet) for about ten days. Then plait them in ropes or hang in nets. If there is a more impressive sight than an onion rope, I've yet to see it!

GIY RECOMMENDED VARIETIES

Centurion, Red Baron, Sturon.

PROBLEMS

Most serious disease is onion white rot which causes leaves to yellow and wilt and bulb gets white mould. No remedy but to remove and burn. You can not grow onions in that spot for up to 7 years.

GIY TIPS

- Baked onions - leave skins on, cut in half and bake for 45 minutes – a revelation!
- If your onions "bolt" and produce a flower spike on the stalk, remove immediately.

MONTHLY INSIGHT– GROWING WITH KIDS

Kids are fantastic GIYers – they are enthusiastic, hard working and they don't have the hang-ups about the process that we adults sometimes do! By growing some food themselves, they gain an increased understanding of where their food comes from, how it's produced and how long it takes. In GIY, we call this food 'empathy'. Numerous studies show that food-growing children are more likely to eat fruits and vegetables, show higher levels of knowledge about nutrition and are more likely to continue healthy eating habits throughout their lives. Food growing can be great exercise for children, getting them off the couch and out in to the fresh air.

Food growing helps children to see that there is a stage before food magically appears in a cellophane wrapper on a supermarket shelf. They learn that food growing is in fact mucky, unpredictable work which they would never guess from the hyper-sanitized, hyper-perfect world presented to them in shops. They figure out that tomatoes aren't in season in January, and that a home-grown fruit or vegetable generally tastes better than it's shop-bought equivalent. I think these are important life lessons.

Any family that has grown their own food will also know that children are more likely to try and eat vegetables that they have had a hand in growing themselves. Our kids become grazers in the veg patch in the summer, walking up and down the rows and sampling vegetables (raw!) that they might turn their noses up to at the kitchen table. I've thought a lot about why this is, and the best I can come up with is that they enjoy tasting the fruits of a project they've been involved in (even on the periphery) and, given the opportunity, children are naturally curious about food.

Below: *Having fun launching our primary schools growing campaign, Sow & Grow*

TOP 5 TIPS FOR GROWING WITH KIDS

1 Kids love sowing seeds (or indeed anything that involves getting their hands dirty). Bigger seeds like those from peas, beans, squashes, pumpkins and courgettes are easier for younger children to handle.

2 Give kids some autonomy in the veg patch– give them a dedicated raised bed or part of a bed for them to experiment with. Let them grow what they want to grow.

3 Encourage them to grow fruit and vegetables that are fast growing so that they see a quick return – radishes are a good example. Runner beans and sunflowers will get tall quickly. Get them to measure themselves against the plants each week!

4 Encourage them to sample crops out in the veg patch – they will love grazing on sweet carrots, tomatoes, strawberries and peas, and it will help develop their palette.

5 In my experience, the top GIY activities for kids are sowing seeds, digging and watering. Basically, the messier the job, the more they will love it. Our eldest will happily water the polytunnel for me, if he's allowed to pick a tomato or strawberry to eat when he's finished!

Left: *Broad bean podding time in the Kelly household.*

Giant pumpkins almost ready for picking.

SEPTEMBER TIPS

PUMPKIN AND SQUASH CARE

Generally you can leave pumpkins and squashes on the plant until October. However you need to keep an eye on the fruit to make sure it does not rot. Raise the fruit up off the ground on to a piece of slate or in a pot so that it is not touching wet soil. Remove leaves near the fruit to allow the sun in on them, which will help with ripening.

When ready, remove fruit with about 7cm of stem left on. They will continue to develop colour after being removed from the plant if left somewhere warm and sunny - a greenhouse, warm windowsill or polytunnel would be ideal.

Stored fruit, once properly "cured" (i.e. skin has firmed up), will last many months. We've had squashes and pumpkins to eat from the 'larder' right up to March or April of the following year. Handle carefully so as not to bruise them.

HARVEST CELERY

Celery doesn't store well in the ground particularly after the first frosts and it doesn't store well out of the ground either. Harvest celery by cutting at ground level - make sure that you do so in such a way as to keep the stems together. Celery will keep for a number of weeks in the fridge and will in fact continue to blanch once picked. Wash in cold water and dry it carefully before putting it in the fridge. Probably the best method of preserving celery is to chop it and freeze - it freezes well but will lose some of its crispness when thawed out. I freeze it in small bags and find it really useful for chucking a handful in to soups, stews or stocks.

SOW WINTER GREENS

As we start to clear crops from the greenhouse/polytunnel, you can use the available space to grow winter salad crops such as lettuce, chard, land cress, corn salad, claytonia (often called purslane or miner's lettuce) and texsel greens. These plants will provide fantastic greens (and bundles of vitamin C) during the winter and if you sow enough of them, they may even keep you in greens until the first new season crops arrive next Spring. They will grow more slowly than they would earlier in the season, but if you sow them now in September, they will put a burst of growth on before the real cold weather sets in. They will also put on a burst of new growth in February/March of the following year.

GROW PEA SHOOTS

You can grow peas specifically to eat the shoots and because you are harvesting the little shoots at just 10-12cm or so high, it's a brilliant fast-growing crop that doesn't need much space and is perfect for container growing. You can grow them pretty much all year round, indoors if you wish, and a single seed tray will yield about a hundred shoots. Simply fill a seed tray with seed compost, water well, and then sprinkle peas generously on top. Arrange them on the surface of the compost so that they are about 2-3cm apart – then push them down in to the compost to about 2cm depth and backfill the little holes with more compost. Place in a bright spot, but not direct sunlight. In about 3-4 weeks harvest with a scissors – you might even get a second harvest from the re-growth.

Onion Tart Tatin

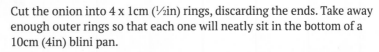

SERVES 8 (MAKES 4)

1 large onion, peeled

100g (4oz) caster sugar

100g (4oz) butter

200g (7oz) ready-rolled puff pastry, thawed if frozen

From *The MacNean Restaurant Cookbook* by Neven Maguire. Gill and Macmillan, 2012.

Cut the onion into 4 x 1cm (½in) rings, discarding the ends. Take away enough outer rings so that each one will neatly sit in the bottom of a 10cm (4in) blini pan.

Sprinkle the sugar over the base of the blini pans. Put two cubes of butter into the base of each one and place a slice of onion on top of each one. Stamp or cut out 4 x 10cm (4in) rounds from the puff pastry and place on top of the onion, carefully tucking down the edges to create a rim. Place in the fridge to rest for at least 10 minutes.

Preheat the oven to 190°C (375°F/gas mark 5).

Place the blini pans directly on the hob on a medium heat and cook for 4–5 minutes to caramelise the sugar. You should be able to see the sugar bubbling up around the edges of the pastry – watch it carefully as it turns from golden to dark brown in colour. Transfer to the oven and cook for another 10 minutes, until the puff pastry is golden brown.

COOK AHEAD

These can be made up to 2 days in advance and kept chilled in the fridge on a plastic tray covered with cling film until needed. To reheat, preheat the oven to 190°C (375°F/gas mark 5), place them on a preheated baking sheet and cook for 6–8 minutes, until heated through.

Leek and Cashel Blue Cheese Tartlet with Balsamic Cherry Tomatoes

DENIS COTTER

SERVES 4

150g plain flour

a large pinch of salt

75g cold butter

40mls cold water

500g leeks

3 cloves of garlic, chopped

1 tablespoon butter

½ teaspoon Dijon mustard

1 tablespoon chopped chives

100g Cashel Blue cheese

400g cherry tomatoes

drizzle of olive oil

2 teaspoons balsamic vinegar

From *Paradiso Seasons* by Denis Cotter.
Published by Atrium, 2003.

Sift the flour and salt together, rub in the butter, add the water and form into a dough. Shape it into a ball with your hands, flatten it gently and chill for at least half an hour.

Roll the pastry and cut out circles to fit four small tartlet cases of about 7cm diameter. Prick the pastry cases all over with a fork and chill them again for 30 minutes, then bake them for eight to ten minutes at 180°C/350°F, until crisp.

Slice the leeks in half lengthways, and wash them well, then slice them thinly.

Melt the butter in a wide pan and cook the leek and garlic over high heat for about five minutes, until the leeks soften. Add the mustard and chives, and cook for one minute more. Season with salt and pepper.

Fill each pastry case three-quarters full with the leeks, and crumble some blue cheese on top. Bake the tartlets at 180°C/350°F for eight to ten minutes, until the leeks have warmed through and the cheese has melted.

Put the cherry tomatoes in a small oven dish and sprinkle with a little olive oil and salt. Roast in the oven for eight to ten minutes, until softened a little, adding the balsamic vinegar for the last minute of cooking. Spoon a pile of roasted tomatoes in their juice on each plate and place a tartlet on top.

Cream of Onion Soup with Apple Juice and Thyme

PAUL FLYNN

You must try this soup. In the restaurant it's our fall back soup. If we have nothing else we always have onions. It's an all year round soup, with a texture of a creamy broth. The long, slow cooking of the onions is essential. This brings out the sweetness and concentrates the flavour. The trick is not to colour the onions at all so you need the lowest heat and a lid on top of the lot to trap the steam and keep the moisture inside.

SERVES 4-6 AS A STARTER OR LIGHT LUNCH

good knob butter

2 large onions, thinly sliced

1 bay leaf

1.5 litres/2¼ pints chicken stock (from a cube will do)

100ml/3½ fl.oz cream

glass apple juice (good quality)

pinch English mustard powder or 1 teaspoon prepared English mustard

pinch chopped fresh thyme

salt and freshly ground black pepper

garlic croutons and grated Cheddar, to serve

From *Second Helpings - Further Irish Adventures with Food* by Paul Flynn. Published by Collins Press. 2005.

Melt the butter in a large heavy-based pan with a tight-fitting lid and once it is foaming, add the onions and bay leaf, stirring to coat. Reduce the heat right down, cover with the lid and cook for 30-40 minutes until the onions are golden brown and caramelised, stirring once or twice.

Pour the stock into the onion mixture and bring to the boil, then reduce the heat and cook gently for another 10 minutes. Add the cream, apple juice, mustard, thyme and season to taste. Allow to just warm through and for all of the flavours to infuse. Ladle into warmed serving bowls and scatter over some garlic croutons and Cheddar to serve.

Ploughman's Chutney

ALYS FOWLER

This one is for those 'gifted' marrows offered up as a bag of courgettes. It is particularly good slathered over turkey on Boxing Day or with strong English Cheddar.

1kg marrow, courgette or pumpkin

a couple of handfuls of salt

500g apples (or green tomatoes) cored, peeled and chopped

500g onions, roughly chopped

250g raisins, sultanas, currants or dried elderberries

500g brown sugar

600ml cider vinegar

3-4 garlic cloves, sliced

2 teaspoons sea salt

2 teaspoons ground ginger

2 teaspoons mustard seeds

pinch of cayenne pepper

FOR THE SPICE BAG

3 teaspoons cloves (around 9 cloves)

1 teaspoon coriander seeds

1 teaspoon black peppercorns

1 cinnamon stick

sterilised jars with lids – how many depends on the size of your jars.

Peel and dice the marrow, courgette or pumpkin, discarding the woody part and any large seeds. Place in a bowl and scatter over a couple of handfuls of salt, just enough so that all surfaces are lightly dusted. Set aside for at least 4 hours (preferably overnight) to draw out all the moisture. Rinse and pat dry. This dry-salting process keeps the marrow in good shape and stops it collapsing, otherwise it just turns to mush.

Make up your spice bag by putting the spices in a piece of muslin and tying them tightly with string. Place all the remaining chutney ingredients in a heavy-based pan and bring to the boil, stirring to dissolve the sugar. Simmer gently, stirring from time to time, until the mixture is thick but not stiff, roughly 40 minutes or so. By the end you should be able to draw a spoon across the bottom of the pan so that it clears, but rapidly refills with syrupy juices.

Ladle the hot chutney into warm sterilised jars, cover with wax discs and put on the lids. Store somewhere cool and dark for at least 2 weeks before using. This chutney will keep well for up to 6 months.

From *Abundance* by Alys Fowler.
Published by Kyle Books, 2013.

Plum Jam

TOM DOORLEY AND JOHANN DOORLEY

When the plums are ripe, we eat them like sweets off the trees – two to three bites and they're gone. Some, though, we will make jam with for scones or morning toast.

MAKES 5-6 JARS

1kg (2lb) plums

300ml (10 fl oz) water

1kg (2lb) sugar

From *Grow and Cook* by Tom Doorley and Johann Doorley. Published by Gill and Macmillan, 2007.

Cut the plums into quarters and remove the stones. Put the pieces of plum and the water into a large saucepan and bring to the boil. Simmer the plums until they are soft. We put the lid on the pan and into the simmering oven of the Aga for 20-30 minutes.

When the plums are soft, add the sugar and stir until dissolved. Turn up the heat and bring to the boil. Put a small plate into the fridge and six jars to sterilise in a low oven at 140°C/285°F/GasMark1. Boil the jam for 10 minutes and check for the setting point. Test for setting by putting a teaspoonful of the jam onto the cold plate in the fridge and letting it cool. If the top of the jam wrinkles when pushed, the jam is ready, otherwise boil the jam for another 5 minutes and try again.

When the jam is ready, take it off the heat and let it cool. After 10 minutes, take the jars out of the oven and pour in the hot jam and seal. Leave to cool and label.

Blackberry & Apple Cobbler

NESSA ROBINS

SERVES 6-8

1 large cooking apple, peeled, cored and thinly sliced

200g blackberries

75g caster sugar

CAKE BATTER

110g butter

110g caster sugar

175g self-raising flour

1 egg

2 tbsp milk

1 tsp vanilla extract

TOPPING

1 tbsp oats

From Nessa Robins
www.nessasfamilykitchen.blogspot.ie

Pre-heat the oven to 200°C/fan 180°C/Gas 6. Grease a medium sized casserole dish, with a little butter.

Line the bottom of the casserole dish with the apple slices and blackberries. Sprinkle over the 75g of sugar.

In a food processor, or mixer, add all of the batter ingredients, apart from the oats, and mix for a few minutes, until well combined.

Spoon the cake batter evenly over the apple and blackberries. Smooth over with a knife and sprinkle over the oats.

Bake in the pre-heated oven for 35-40 minutes, until the pudding has risen, is golden in colour and cooked through. Serve hot or cold with custard, cream or vanilla ice-cream.

Mam's Apple Tart

Mam is my beloved mother. A famously reluctant cook, she was, however, a dab hand at the apple tarts, and could make them in her sleep. This is utterly delicious and brought memories of childhood rushing back.

SERVES 6

FOR THE PASTRY

170g plain flour

55g icing sugar

110g butter, chilled and cut into cubes

1 egg yolk

FOR THE FILLING

5 cooking apples, peeled, cored and chopped

4 cloves and 1 cinnamon stick*

2 tablespoons caster sugar

FOR THE GLAZE

1 egg, lightly beaten (or milk)

caster sugar

*Obviously my mother didn't use such stuff. Any Irish woman found adding flavouring to food in the 1960s could have been stripped of her citizenship.

Grease a 20cm pie tin.

You can make this pastry in your food processor if you're lucky enough to have one. Sieve the flour and icing sugar together, then add the butter. Beat slowly until the mix goes sandy and there are no lumps of butter still visible. Add the egg yolk and mix again. The pastry should gradually cohere, i.e. start looking like pastry. If it still looks dry and crumbly (this is unlikely) add a tablespoon of cold water and mix again.

Wrap the lump of pastry in cling film, then put in the fridge for at least an hour.

Meanwhile, put the chopped cooking apples into a heavy-bottomed saucepan. (To be quite honest, I didn't know you could even get cooking apples any more. I thought they were something from the olden days.)

Bash the cloves (this releases their oil) and add to the apples along with the cinnamon stick. Add the caster sugar and 2 tablespoons water and stew over a gentle heat. However, to quote Mam here, 'Go aisy! You don't want the apples to turn to mush.'

When the apples are soft but still lumpy – this should take about 20 minutes – test for sweetness. If you think they're a bit sour, add more sugar.

Preheat the oven to 170°C/325°F/gas 3.

Now, for the 'cling film method' of rolling out pastry. Take the pastry out of the fridge and remove the cling film. Divide the pastry into two 'halves', one slightly bigger than the other. Shape the bigger half into a round, then place on a piece of cling film, about 30cm by 30cm. Place another piece of cling film – roughly the same size as the first one – on top of the pastry, then use your rolling pin to flatten the pastry. To confirm, your pastry is enveloped between both pieces of cling film and your rolling pin is rolling over the top piece. I'm sorry if this is confusing. The thing is, it's actually a useful thing to get the hang of because the cling film will 'hold' the pastry so that it's less likely to break as you roll it out.

So roll the pastry, then turn the whole cling-filmed parcel 90 degrees and roll again, and so on, until your pastry is roughly the right size and shape to line your tin. You might think, 'Feck this cling film malarkey', it's far too much trouble, and if so, then stop. I don't want to add to your woes, only reduce them.

Right, now the tricky bit, getting the pastry into the tin. Remove the top layer of cling film. Place your rolling pin horizontally across the dough and using it almost as a hinge, fold the pastry in two and lift it off the bottom layer of cling film – do this very quickly, this is not a time to start staring thoughtfully into the distance and musing on existential matters – then lower it into the tin.

Things might go pear-shaped on you – they did for me, my pastry 'broke' – but don't panic. What I did was assemble a 'patchwork' pastry case. I put the biggest unbroken piece into the tin, then used the next-biggest piece to cover more of the tin, overlapping the joins slightly. I kept doing this until the tin was fully lined, then I pressed my fingers along the joins until they had all but disappeared.

Even if your pastry doesn't fully break, holes may develop and there's no shame in this, no shame at all. Just patch the holes with more pastry and move on.

Trim the edges with a sharp knife, then add in the stewed apple. Yes, that's right, no baking blind on this tart. Mam sounded extremely surprised when I suggested it. She's never done it – probably because she was so busy – but the tarts never suffered. It means that the bottom layer of pastry stays soft and crumbly, instead of crunchy, but no less delicious for it.

Roll out the second 'half' of pastry using whichever method appeals to you, then drape it over the top of the tart. Stick the edge of the bottom layer against the edge of the top layer, using the egg wash or milk.

Swipe the top layer with the egg wash or milk and prick several times with a fork. Bake for about 30 minutes, until the pastry is golden brown.

Scatter caster sugar over the top just before serving.

From *Saved by Cake* by Marian Keyes. Published by Michael Joseph 2012.

THIS MONTH'S TOP JOBS

* Pot up herbs for indoor winter use.

* Clean up beds as you clear crops.

* Find a good source of farmyard manure.

* Start storing root crops like carrots and beetroot.

October

I WAS ABOUT 5 HOURS IN TO MY monster 8-hour 'pickle-athon' and up to my neck in diced fruit, veg and vinegar syrups. I had just peeled, cored and chopped 2kg of pears, and a pan of boiling, sugary stickiness had just overflowed on the stove. The kitchen looked like a bomb had hit it. The kids were still in their school uniforms and dinner was chronically late. I was tired, cranky, sweaty and hungry (ironic, given that I was surrounded by mounds of food). It was at that moment that Mrs Kelly chose to arrive in from the garden with another enormous bucket of windfall pears and a big smile on her face. "Look what else I found," she said, beaming at what was surely an entire winter's supply of overripe fruit. "That's great," I deadpanned, without much conviction, before turning away and muttering something unprintable.

At this time of the year, many types of vegetables and fruit are in serious glut territory, and suspended in that perilous no-man's land between abundance and waste. So you have to move fast - do something with them so you can eat them later in the year, or lose them forever to the compost heap. That means making a conscious decision to dedicate the time required to make a jam, pickle or chutney, or whatever other preserving recipes you have in your arsenal.

Put aside any romantic notions about how the hours spent peeling, dicing and chopping will make you a better person. Let's be honest, it can be just hard bloody work. But the upside – ah the upside! That wonderful, primordial smug/satisfied feeling that arises the day after a mammoth session of food storing. Gazing along the rows of jam and Kilner jars, you can congratulate yourself on a job well done and dream of a day in the near-distant future, when fresh produce is starting to wear thin, and you can pop open a jar and taste the harvest all over again.

Things to Do in... *October*

PREPARATION

Pot up herbs so that they can be grown inside for use during winter. Continue to lift crops that have finished harvesting and clean up the beds. By now, green manures sown in late summer will be ready to be dug in to the soil. You can also sow over-wintering green manures now. Try and find a good source of farmyard manure if you don't have your own – cow, horse, pig, sheep and chicken manure are all great sources of nutrients for your soil. If you are going to cover empty beds down with manure (or homemade garden compost) for the winter, the earlier you do it the better. October or early November is ideal.

TO DO LIST

Pull up crops which have finished harvesting and compost. Plant fruit trees and bushes. Tidy away canes and supports that you used for your peas, beans etc. and you should be able to use them next year. Leave them in the ground or throw them in a corner, and you probably won't. Start collecting fallen leaves for leaf mould. Start storing vegetables like carrots and beets in boxes of sand – only store the perfect specimens. Try to process the rest. Check apples regularly to see if they are ripe – early ripening apples generally don't store that well. Cut autumn-fruiting raspberry canes down to the ground.

SOWING SEEDS AND PLANTING OUT

You can sow hardy varieties of peas and broad beans later this month for an early spring crop but only do so in well-drained soil. You could also plant selected varieties of garlic and winter onion sets. The former will benefit from a good frost so it's traditional to plant before Christmas. I always hold off until spring to sow my garlic, onions, beans and peas. What can I say, I am basically lazy and appreciate the break..

Right: *Sliced cucumbers ready for pickling.*

Left: *Champion pumpkin grower.*

HARVESTING – WHAT'S IN SEASON?

The harvest should still be in full swing this month. It's also a month when you are still harvesting many of the great autumn fruit and vegetables – pumpkins, squashes, courgette, apples, pears etc. Continue to harvest wild mushrooms, elderberry, blackberries, sloes, peas, French and runner beans, tomatoes, cucumbers, aubergines, peppers, chilli-peppers, celery, leeks, cabbage. Your root crops like carrots, parsnips, swedes, celeriac, turnips and beetroots, as well as your main crop potatoes should still be thriving. You can leave these in the ground for another while yet and use them as you need them, or lift and store if you prefer. Start to fall back in love again with old winter reliables such as kale, chard and spinach. They will shortly become your very best friends.

Veg of the Month - *Beetroot*

WHY GROW IT?

Many people have an aversion to beetroot because the only way they have ever tasted it is boiled and drowned in vinegar! If this is your experience, it deserves a second chance for it is a fine crop, which (1) you can grow a lot of in a small space, (2) is easy to grow, (3) can be eaten all year round since it stores well, (4) is incredibly good for you and (5) has multiple uses – boil it, bake it, grate it raw in to salads and slaws; make chutneys, wine and even cakes (beetroot brownies, yum). Try baking young, small beets in tinfoil parcels – they are a revelation.

SOWING

Many people sow their beetroot direct – being contrary, I always sow mine in module trays in the potting shed for transplanting later. I always find it more successful to plant out a hardy seedling rather than sowing a tiny seed direct in the soil. I sow one seed per module about 2cm deep. Bear in mind that a beetroot seed is actually a "cluster" of seeds, so you may need to thin out if they all germinate. I let just one seedling grow on in each module, gently removing the others and discarding them.

About a month later, I plant the seedlings outside (though my first sowing of the year is planted out in the polytunnel). The seedlings are planted 10cm apart in rows 25cm apart. This means that in a 1m x 1m bed you will get 40 beetroot – that's a lot of food from a small space. I do three sowings of beetroot each year. The first in February is planted in the polytunnel in March and ready in late May. The second sowing is in late April for summer eating. The final sowing is in June for winter storage (lifting in October). I aim to grow about 150 beetroot between the three sowings.

GROWING

Keep the ground weed free by hoeing carefully. Young beets are sensitive to cold spells which is why we generally wait until April for the first outdoor crop. Protect young seedlings with fleece if required. Overwatering encourages leaf growth at the expense of root formation.

HARVESTING

Start to harvest when they are golf ball size – leaving every second one behind to fully mature. Do not let beets grow larger than a tennis ball. You can also harvest the leaves for salads but not too many as the root needs the leaves too. Lift July-sown crop in October and store in a box of sand (horticultural or play sand) – they will keep for 3-4 months. Twist off leaves a few centimetres above the root before storing. Handle carefully – they will "bleed" if damaged.

GIY RECOMMENDED VARIETIES

Detroit Globe, Boltardy, Chioggia, Bulls Blood.

PROBLEMS

Beetroot is generally trouble free but black bean aphid can occasionally be troublesome.

GIY TIPS

- Soak seeds in warm water for 20 minutes before sowing to aid germination.
- Beetroot doesn't like dry soil and it causes "woody" roots (very unpleasant). Keep soil moist in dry weather and/or mulch to conserve moisture.

Right: *Beetroot-pick 'em small for best flavour.*

MONTHLY INSIGHT – CROP ROTATION

WHAT ON EARTH IS CROP ROTATION?

Crop rotation is a fancy term for grouping similar vegetables together and moving them around each year to prevent a build-up of pests/disease and to maximise soil fertility. The groupings generally have the same or similar nutrient requirements and keeping them together means that you can more easily provide them with the best growing conditions – for example the brassica family (cabbage, kale etc.) prefer a slightly alkaline soil and you can therefore put lime in the bed where they are to be planted to reduce acidity. You can divide your vegetable patch in to areas and move the veg families around to different areas. Or, if you grow in raised beds you can allocate a raised bed (or several raised beds) to each family. Draw a plan of your beds and write down where you planted things so that you can refer to it the following year. No, you won't remember!

MY FIVE YEAR CROP ROTATION

There are loads of different crop rotation 'schemes' and it doesn't really matter which you pick, as long as you follow the general prinicple of moving veg around your patch to prevent the build up of disease. Don't get too stressed about the whole thing. The usual form is to grow your brassicas in the area or bed where you grew legumes the previous year because they love the nitrogen that plants like broad beans and peas have 'fixed' in to the soil the previous year. Root vegetables do not require a lot of nitrogen and therefore will do well if planted where the brassicas were last year. The system I use divides vegetables in to five groups, which I then rotate around five areas of the veg patch. It comes with a handy mnemonic to help me remember it: *People Love Bunches of Roses*. The five families are:

Potatoes (People) – early and main crop spuds.

Legumes (Love) – peas, broad beans, French beans, runner beans.

Brassicas (Bunches) – kale, cabbage, cauliflower, kohlrabi, radish, Brussels Sprouts, swede, turnips etc.

Onions (Of) – onions, leeks, garlic and shallots.

Roots (Roses) – parsnips, carrots, beetroot, fennel, celery/celeriac.

All the other vegetables get shoved in where I have the space. Courgettes, squashes, pumpkins and sweetcorn I generally add in to the legume area. Some vegetables like globe artichokes and rhubarb are a more permanent fixture in one location, so I just work around them. So the five -year plan looks like this:

	BED/AREA 1	BED/AREA 2	BED/AREA 3	BED/AREA 4	BED/AREA 5
YEAR 1	Potatoes	Legumes	Brassicas	Onions	Roots
YEAR 2	Legumes	Brassicas	Onions	Roots	Potatoes
YEAR 3	Brassicas	Onions	Roots	Potatoes	Legumes
YEAR 4	Onions	Roots	Potatoes	Legumes	Brassicas
YEAR 5	Roots	Potatoes	Legumes	Brassicas	Onions

We filmed a series of GIY videos with growing guru Klaus Laitenberger at his home in Milkwood Farm. We filmed this shot to explain crop rotation.

OCTOBER TIPS

RIPENING GREEN TOMS

A good way to ripen green toms is to place them in a tray and put them in a drawer. Next to them place a couple of ripe apples which will generate the ripening gas ethylene which will help them ripen. Ripe tomatoes will keep in the fridge for about a week in a polythene bag.

SHREDDING FOR GREAT COMPOST

Small garden shredders are available quite cheaply from most garden centres - they are a great investment for improving your compost heap. Chances are you have a huge amount of foliage available from your veggie patch to go on your compost heap at the moment (cabbage plants, pea and bean plants etc.). These make fine additions to the compost heap, but shredding them first means they will decompose much faster. If you don't have a shredder use a shears to cut up large leaves, and use a sledgehammer to bash down large brassica stems (and you can cancel your gym membership!).

SAVE BEANS

If you are removing runner and French bean plants, don't throw out pods that look past their best. You can harvest a crop of 'haricot' beans from within the pods for use later in the winter. Leave the pods on the plant until they turn yellow/brown and then hang the plants indoors to dry. When the pods are brittle, remove the beans from inside and dry them on a sheet of paper for a few days. Then store in an airtight container.

BRASSICA CARE

A bit of care on over-wintering brassicas (cabbages, Brussels sprouts, purple sprouting broccoli etc.) now will ensure healthy, thriving plants. Give a good weed around the plants and remove any yellowing leaves, which are no use to the plant and can encourage botrytis. Earth up around the base of the plants - this will help them survive heavy winter winds. Caterpillars are still a problem – check the leaves regularly for them and remove any that you see.

FREEZING BERRIES

Frozen berries will lose some structure when thawed but they're still ideal for making smoothies and fruit crumbles/pies, or for sprinkling on your porridge or muesli. Spread them on a single layer on a baking tray or sheet to freeze - when they are well frozen, gather them up and pop them in a zip lock freezer bag.

Spiced Beetroot and Potato Rosti

SERVES 6
(MAKES 12 ROSTI)

250g Greek yoghurt

2 tbsp pomegranate molasses

800g precooked beetroot, roughly grated

1.3kg potatoes (Rooster or similar), peeled and roughly grated

2 tbsp salt

4 cloves garlic, crushed

6 tbsp olive oil

4 tsp ground cumin

freshly ground black pepper

4 tbsp chopped chives

6 eggs

From *Dream Deli* by Lilly Higgins.
Published by Gill and Macmillan 2013.

Preheat the oven to 200°C. Line 2 baking trays with greaseproof paper.

Place the yoghurt in a bowl and gently stir through the molasses. Cover and refrigerate.

Place a tea towel in a colander and sit it into the sink. Tip the grated beetroot and potatoes into the tea towel and sprinkle the salt over. Gather all four corners of the towel and squeeze the bundle to get as much liquid out as possible. Leave to sit for 5 minutes before squeezing again. Try to get the mixture as dry as possible. Shake the vegetables out of the towel and place them in a large bowl with the garlic, olive oil, cumin, black pepper and chives. Stir to combine.

Place 6 mounds of the potato mix on each tray. Use a circular biscuit cutter to achieve a uniform shape if it helps. Usually the rougher the edges, the crispier it becomes. Don't pack the mixture down tightly, as it won't cook evenly. Leave the mixture a little loose and it will settle as it cooks.

Place the trays in the oven to bake for 40–45 minutes, rotating halfway through, until the rosti are crisp and golden. Serve immediately with the yoghurt and a fried egg on top.

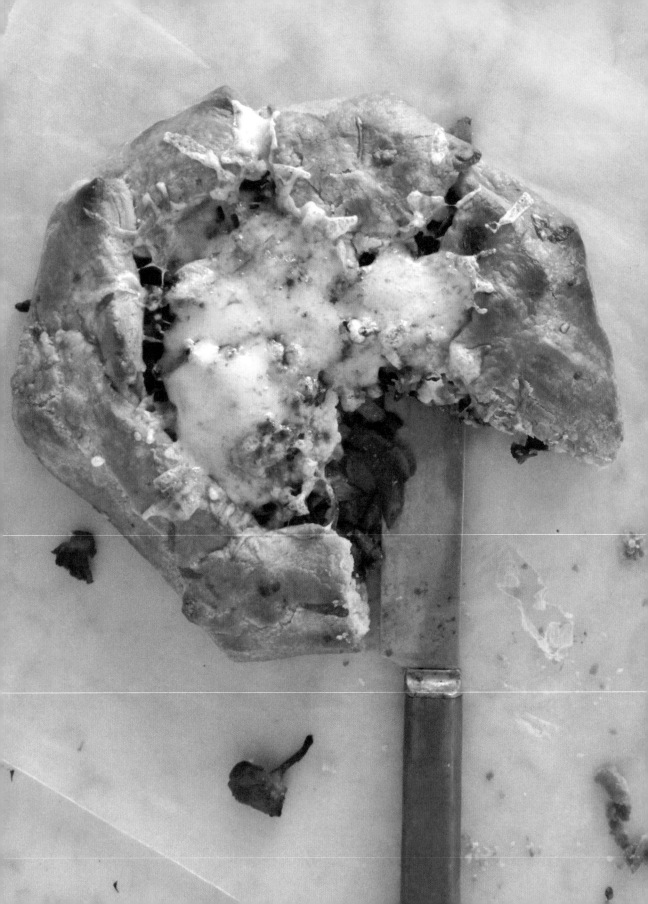

Wild Chanterelle, Caramelised Onion, Caraway & Buffalo Cheese Galette

IMEN MCDONNELL

SERVES 4

2 teaspoons olive oil

1 large sweet onion, cut in half and thinly sliced into half moons

450g/16oz chanterelle mushrooms (or any wild mushrooms)

handful of fresh caraway, chopped coarsely (can sub thyme or other fresh herbs that you love)

salt

ground black pepper

85g/3oz grated Toonsbridge Dairy buffalo hard cheese or a similar hard cheese

milk, for brushing

FOR THE SHORTCRUST PASTRY

1 ½ cups standard plain flour

½ cup butter

pinch of sea salt

¼ cup cold water

From Imen McDonnell from her blog www.farmette.ie

To make the shortcrust pastry, place flour, butter and salt in large mixing bowl. Using your fingertips, gently rub ingredients together until they resemble rough breadcrumbs. Do not over mix or the butter will begin to melt from the heat of your fingers. Add water and mix until a dough is formed. Cover with cling film and refrigerate for 30 minutes or overnight. Gently re-work pastry before using, taking care to ensure it remains cold and firm.

Preheat oven to 230°C / 450°F.

Add 1 teaspoon of oil to a large sauté pan over medium heat. Add onion, salt and pepper, tossing to coat evenly. Cook 20 minutes, stirring often, until onions have softened and turned a lovely shade of golden caramel. Remove onions to a bowl and set aside.

Add remaining teaspoon of oil and add mushrooms, caraway, a little more salt and pepper. Toss to coat. Cook, stirring occasionally, until mushrooms have turned brown and released most of their liquid. Remove pan from heat and pour mushrooms onto a paper-towel lined plate in order to remove as much moisture as possible from them.

On a lightly floured surface, roll out shortcrust and transfer to a parchment-lined large rimmed baking sheet. Leaving a 2 to 3-inch border around the centre, spread out half of the onions on the dough. Layer with mushrooms and caraway mix, evenly distributing, and finish with remaining onions. Sprinkle with a little more pepper. Top with the shredded cheese. Fold in sides of the dough circle roughly, pressing slightly to adhere pieces to one another. Brush edges of dough with milk.

Bake for 25 to 30 minutes, until crust is golden and cheese is bubbling. Garnish with remaining fresh caraway. Remove and allow to rest for 5 minutes before cutting into slices.

Imen McDonnell with family.

Pickled Pears

DARINA ALLEN

Pears are in season in autumn, although you can make this pickle at other times of the year with shop-bought pears. It is particularly delicious with smoked duck, watercress and blue cheese salad, venison or pigeon.

MAKES 6 X 450G (1LB) POTS

1.8kg (4lb) pears (Conference or Doyenne de Comice are perfect, but Bartlett pears will also suffice)

juice and zest of 1 organic lemon

600ml (1 pint) of white wine vinegar

30ml (1fl oz) sherry vinegar (optional)

600g (1¼ lb) sugar

2.5cm (1in) piece of fresh ginger, peeled and sliced

1 cinnamon stick

2 star anise

4 cloves

From *Forgotten Skills of Cooking* by Darina Allen. Published by Kyle Books, 2010.

Peel, core and quarter the pears and put them into a stainless-steel saucepan. Remove the lemon zest with a swivel-top peeler, squeeze the juice over the fruit and toss well.

Cover and cook on a gentle heat while you prepare the pickle.

Put the vinegars, sugar, spices, and lemon zest into a stainless-steel saucepan. Bring to the boil, stirring until all the sugar is dissolved.

Simmer for 5 minutes, then add the pears and continue to cook until the pears are completely soft – about 10-30 minutes, depending on the variety and degree of ripeness.

Fill the pears into sterilised jars, while continuing to cook the liquid.

Pour the boiling liquid over the pears, making sure they are well covered. Seal and, if possible, leave for a couple of weeks to mellow before tucking in!

Pumpkin Chutney

MARTIJN KAJUITER

Chutney combines well with rich dishes such as braised meat, grilled fatty fish and, of course, cheese.

MAKES 2 JARS

700g pumpkin, skin and seeds removed, diced into equal cubes

250g apple, grated

1 tbsp fresh ginger, grated

¼ chilli pepper, finely chopped

200ml vinegar

60g brown sugar

20g jam sugar

1 tsp coriander seeds

½ tsp cloves, crushed

½ tsp black peppercorns, crushed

¼ cinnamon stick

2 star anise

juice and zest of 1 lemon

salt to taste

From *Cliffhouse Hotel – The Cookbook*, by Martijn Kajuiter. Published by Houghton Mifflin Harcourt Trade 2010.

Put the pumpkin, apple, vinegar and the chilli into a large pot. Add 2 cups of water and bring to the boil.

Turn down the heat and after 45 minutes add the spices and the sugar. Let the chutney simmer until the pumpkin starts to shine and fall apart.

Add the ginger, lemon juice and zest. Simmer for a further 25 minutes, adding water if it becomes too dry.

Season to taste. Spoon into clean preserve jars and seal. Turn the jars upside down in order to create a vacuum.

Turn right side up after 10 minutes and store in a dark and cool place.

The chutney needs to mature for about 2 weeks before it is good to eat, but it can hold for up to a year. After opening, keep it in the fridge.

Steamed Pak Choi with Green Chilli, Ginger and Peanut Dressing

JOY LARKCOM

SERVES 2-4

4 small or 2 medium-sized pak choi

1 green chilli, deseeded and thinly sliced

2 teaspoons grated fresh ginger

2 tablespoons roasted peanuts, coarsely chopped

4 tablespoons olive oil

rind and juice of 1 lime

2 tablespoons soy sauce

a few drops of toasted sesame oil

From *Oriental Vegetables* by Joy Larkcom.
Published by Frances Lincoln 2007.

Halve or quarter the pak choi lengthways. Steam for 3-4 minutes. Meanwhile, fry the chilli, ginger and peanuts in 2 tablespoons of the olive oil for a minute. Transfer to a bowl and stir in the rest of the ingredients and the remaining olive oil. Place the pak choi in a serving dish and pour the dressing over. Serve warm.

Baked Spiced Plums with Oatcakes

PAUL FLYNN

SERVES 4

FOR THE SPICED PLUMS

8 plums

3 pears

100g butter

75g brown sugar

pinch mixed spice

sprig of thyme

FOR THE OATCAKES

225g butter

110g flour

200g jumbo oats

80g sugar

From Paul Flynn, *Tannery Restaurant*, Dungarvan, Co Waterford

Cut the plums in half and place in a roasting dish. Peel and cut the pears and add to the dish.

Scatter the butter, sugar, mixed spice and thyme. Bake at 170°C for 20 minutes or until the fruit is just soft.

To make the oatcakes

Cream the butter and sugar. Add the dry ingredients and mix until combined. Roll into cylinders with cling film. Slice and bake at 180°C for 8 to 10 minutes.

Chocolate and Beetroot Brownie with a Golden Beetroot and Carrageen Mousse

Beetroot Brownies are one of our top sellers at GROW HQ, and since we have a constant supply of beetroot from the veg patch, we can serve them all year round. They are velvety and absolutely delicious.

MAKES 6-10 PORTIONS

BROWNIE

150g grated cooked beetroot

20g chopped beetroot leaf stalks

150g butter

150g dark chocolate drops

2 eggs

150g sugar

90g flour

30g flax seed (or sesame, or pumpkin)

MOUSSE

200g cooked & peeled golden beetroots

50ml water

40g caster sugar

50ml whipped cream

5g dried carrageen

JB Dubois is Head Chef at GROW HQ.

First make your mousse. Soak the dried carrageen in a bowl of cold water for 20 to 30 minutes. Puree finely the cooked beetroot with the sugar in a food processor. Strain the soaked carrageen and squeeze the excess water. Simmer the carrageen with 50 ml of water in a small sauce pan for 15 minutes. Pass through a fine sieve, squeezing all the seaweed with a spoon. Incorporate the seaweed gel with the beetroot puree and fold in the whipped cream. Pour the mix straight away into small silicon moulds (ice cube trays can do the job perfectly). Leave set in the fridge for 3 to 4 hours before de-moulding and serving.

Next up, make your brownies. Preheat the oven to 160°. Melt the chocolate and the butter in a glass bowl over some boiling water. Whisk the eggs with the sugar in a second mixing bowl for 3 minutes and incorporate the melted chocolate mix in to the egg mix.

Fold in the sieved flour then fold in the grated cooked beetroots and the chopped beetroot stalks. Pour the brownie mix in to a greased baking pan (approx. 22cm x 22cm). Sprinkle the seeds over the top and bake for 35 minutes. Serve lukewarm with the mousse on top.

Upside Down Pear Tart

Apples and pears are the harbingers of winter. They are also the basis of lots of delicious hearty dishes that help us to cope with the change in the season and the hard weather to come. Autumn is a time when the emphasis changes in the kitchen and we leave behind some of the lighter, almost ethereal, dishes of summer and turn towards something more earthy, maybe less refined.

Even though this is basically a simple dish, the recipe is all about patience and really first class ingredients. At *The Cliff House* we make individual tarts but at home I would suggest making a big one to share with family or friends.

The best tartes tatins are made, cooked and eaten at once, served with a generous scoop of vanilla ice cream and a dash of Baileys. You don't hang around with this dish.

SERVES 6-8

1 sheet of puff pastry, cut into a round the size of the pan

5 medium-sized pears, peeled, cored and quartered

200g sugar (mixed with seeds of ½ vanilla pod, ½ tsp each of ground nutmeg and cardamom)

50g butter

70ml water

zest of 1 lemon

You will need a non-stick frying pan with a 24cm base.

From *Cliff House Hotel – The Cookbook* by Martijn Kajuiter. Published by Houghton Mifflin Harcourt Trade 2010.

Pre-heat the oven to 175°C.

Add the sugar mix to the water in the pan. Dissolve on a medium heat and then let it come to the point of caramelisation.

Add the butter and pears and soften them slowly on a low heat, turning the pears so they are cooked on both sides. Make sure the pears are round side down in the caramel and arrange them evenly in the pan.

Cover with the pastry and press and mould it tight around the pears. Then bake until the pastry crust is brown and crisp.

Remove from the oven and place a large plate on top of the pan/pie. Turn it upside down very quickly and remove the pan to reveal the tarte.

Sprinkle the top (which was, until recently, the bottom) with lemon zest.

Cut into slices and serve directly with vanilla ice cream and Baileys Irish Cream.

November

THERE'S A MOMENT IN EVERY GIYER'S year when things pivot from a focus on the current year to preparing for the next. It always amazes me how suddenly it happens. So, imagine this scene. It's November, and I am out in the veg patch at my happiest, clearing a raised bed in which I grew squashes, pumpkins, sweetcorn and beans that year – harvesting the last of the produce, removing the dead/dying plants and getting them on to the compost heap, putting away the canes that the runner beans grew up, and turning over the soil with a fork to clean up the beds.

As I work, I start to think about what would be growing in the bed the following year, so I head for the potting shed where I have a notebook in which I plan my crop rotation – that sounds far more organized than it really is. My 'planning' involves no more than a basic sketch of the veg patch so I can map out a five-year rotation (with the patch divided roughly in to five areas, one for each major veg family). Having spent 10 minutes doodling, to work out broadly what's going to go where next year, I find myself standing in the veg patch again, imagining what will be in each location, and thinking about the soil requirements and the work to be done on each area over the winter.

I have long since lost sight of the job I was there to do, and am basically in daydreaming mode – thinking about next year's growing, the blank canvass of opportunity stretching out ahead of me. The focus has moved on again and another year of growing suddenly beckons.

THIS MONTH'S TOP JOBS

* Plant garlic, broad beans and winter onion sets.

* Divide rhubarb plants.

* Earth up cabbage and Brussels sprouts.

* Prune apple trees.

Things to Do in... *November*

PREPARATION

Thoughts really are now starting to turn to next year's growing. If you are planning to cover down your beds for the winter (which will keep the worst of the bad weather off them, suppress weeds and prevent the rain from leaching nutrients from the soil), you need to get working on it. It's also a good time to prepare new ground for spring. Buy yourself a good spade. Or alternatively try cutting back the grass, then cover the area with about five layers of newspaper and then a layer of compost. Next Spring you should be able to dig straight into this new patch and prepare it for planting. Start investigating seed catalogues for next year.

TO DO LIST

'Earth up' vegetables that will be buffeted by the winds and storms over the winter such as cabbage, cauliflower and particularly Brussels sprouts. Tie Brussels sprouts and sprouting broccoli to canes and apply mulch. Continue to tidy up beds, removing crops, digging in green manures etc. Divide up your rhubarb if you want to propagate and cover it with a thick mulch of manure. If you grow perennial herbs outside, it's a good idea to move them to a sheltered spot. Continue to weed ground dug over since a crop has been removed – they say 'One year's seeding makes seven years' weeding'! Prune apple trees – you are aiming for a goblet-shaped open tree. Prune any crossed and damaged branches, and those that are growing in towards the centre of the tree. The key is to improve circulation of air around the tree. Don't over prune as this will mean much leafy growth next year and little fruit.

SOWING SEEDS AND PLANTING OUT

As per last month's calendar you can sow broad beans outside now for an early crop

Top right: *Garlic braid hanging in the kitchen.*

Middle right: *Herbs brought inside for the winter.*

next spring. It's important to use over-winter varieties such as Aquadulce. To avoid broad beans seeds rotting before germination, make small newspaper cups and germinate them indoors first. Next summer's garlic does best if it's planted before Christmas – plant outdoors in well-prepared soil in a sunny spot. Some varieties of onion sets can over-winter and will be ready to harvest in early summer. Again choose a well-drained soil, otherwise they will rot. Keep an eye on them for frost heave.

HARVESTING – WHAT'S IN SEASON?

Early frosts can kill off tender vegetables but you can continue to harvest perpetual spinach, cabbage, cauliflower, potatoes, swede, parsnips, apples and pears. Start harvesting leeks (very tasty if cut really fine and sautéed in some butter), winter cabbage, kale, artichokes, Brussels sprouts. Time to lift carrots and turnips or at least cover them with a good layer of straw to keep them warm.

Veg of the Month - *Carrots*

WHY GROW IT?

Perhaps not quite for the beginner, carrots are difficult enough to grow and require a deep, light, stone free, fertile soil to do well. But if you get the soil right, you will be rewarded with a crunchy, sweet and flavoursome crop which will store well. Carrots are the classic stockpot vegetable and are full of vitamin A.

SOWING

Carrots are best sown direct in the soil as they do not transplant well. Never add fresh manure when sowing carrots as it will cause them to fork, and encourage leafy growth. You can however add well rotted manure the previous autumn to the area where you will grow carrots. I mainly practice 'no dig' growing in my veg patch, but I always dig the bed where my carrots are going in the early spring to make sure there is at least a spade's depth of good friable soil – compacted soil equals stunted carrots.

Carrot seeds are tiny so this is one situation where you will really need to get the seed bed to a 'fine tilth'. I do just two sowings of carrots each year: an early sowing in the polytunnel in March and then my main crop carrots in late May or early June – this seems late, but germination is better at this time of the year and you also avoid the worst of the carrot root fly. I make shallow (2cm) trenches with a draw hoe or the handle of a rake (tidying the trench up with my hands) and then sow the carrot seeds. In a standard bed, I will get about 4-5 rows of carrots (20cm apart). Having sown the seeds, I then use the rake to cover the seeds in the trench. Keep the seed bed moist to encourage germination. Don't be alarmed if nothing seems to be happening! It could take 2-3 weeks. Thin to 5cm spacing when the seedlings are large enough to handle. Remove weeds carefully.

GROWING

Carrots dislike competition from weeds so keep the bed weed free – use a hoe along the rows and hand-weed around the carrots. Carrots don't need a lot of watering, but in very dry weather keep the soil moist. A good way to think about growing carrots is that you want the roots to reach down in to the soil for nutrients and water, because it will mean longer roots. So, be frugal with your watering and feeding!

HARVESTING

Baby carrots will be ready about 7 weeks after sowing, and you can leave the rest behind to grow more (maincrop varieties take about 11 weeks). Lift by hand, or ease out with a fork carefully if ground is hard. Lift carrots rather than leaving them in the ground to grow too large – they are not too tasty when very big. Lift maincrop carrots in October and store in boxes of sand – they can be left in the soil if growth has stopped, but I find they are vulnerable to slug damage so I always lift them.

GIY RECOMMENDED VARIETIES

Amsterdam Forcing, Chantenay Red, Autumn King.

PROBLEMS

If blight is the bogeyman for spuds, then the carrot root fly is the same for carrots – this menace lays eggs in the soil around the carrots, and the little maggots tunnel in to roots which then rot. Delaying your sowing until late May will help. Alternatively, cover the bed completely with bionet or put a 60cm barrier of fine mesh around the entire carrot bed. Be careful when thinning – the fly is attracted to the scent of the broken foliage.

GIY TIPS

- The main thing to watch out for with failed germination is seed falling down between clumps of soil and therefore being too deep to germinate. A fine tilth seedbed should prevent this.
- Some GIYers have reported success with sowing carrots in toilet roll inserts – the seed is sown indoors or under cover in an insert full of compost and then when the seedlings have developed, you plant the whole thing (insert and all) in to a hole in the ground. Using this method you avoid tampering with the root. Personally this seems like a lot of hard work for an individual carrot!

MONTHLY INSIGHT– FRUIT

I like to think I've picked up a fair bit of expertise when it comes to growing vegetables over the years, but I always feel a little less sure of myself when it comes to fruit and I have to confess that I'm nowhere near self-sufficient. Having said that, by focussing on a small number of fairly reliable tree and soft fruits, I manage to get away with it and produce a fairly decent amount of fruit from the garden.

I have seven apple trees, planted at different stages over our ten years here – they are inexpertly pruned, but starting to come in to their own. We have two wonderful pear trees – they took a number of years to get going, but over the last few years have provided bountiful fruit (poached pears in syrup are my new favourite thing). Our plum tree also crops amazingly well, always a surprise to me in this climate.

In the veg patch I grow (often badly) rhubarb, raspberries, strawberries, blackcurrants, gooseberries and blueberries. We are also lucky that our garden is surrounded by a wild blackthorn and blackberry hedge so we don't have to go far for blackberry or sloe picking.

GIY'S TOP 5 HOMEGROWN FRUIT

1 Apples – Did you know that 9 out of every 10 apples sold in Irish supermarkets are imported? Even one or two apple trees will provide a huge amount of your own apples. You can now buy miniature apple trees so even the smallest garden can produce a decent crop of apples.

2 Plums – grow surprisingly well in our climate and produce an abundance of plump, succulent fruits. Will any of them make it to the kitchen?

3 Strawberries – the true taste of summer, strawberries are easy to grow and can even be grown in containers. A strawberry plant will produce good fruit for about three years, making it a wise investment. And kids will just love them.

4 Raspberries – raspberries grow on tall canes and therefore need some space, but they reward the GIYer with their sheer lusciousness! I grow autumn varieties which are reliable and easy to maintain.

5 Rhubarb – A single rhubarb crown will provide delicious stems for years to come. It's typically the first new season crop of the year (in April), arriving before other spring vegetables, and therefore much appreciated.

NOVEMBER TIPS

LOVE YOUR POLYTUNNEL

It's a good time of the year to tidy up the potting shed, greenhouse or polytunnel - clean away pots, trays and old canes etc. Washing the plastic in your polytunnel will help it to last longer (it can last 10-15 years if you mind it) and by removing any green mould you allow more light in which is good for next year's veggies. Use a little bit of washing up liquid in warm water and a long-handled soft brush. You will probably need a ladder to clean the top of the polytunnel. The same washing regime is good for the glass on your greenhouse.

SEAWEED FORAGING

To some it's just a slimy mess, but to GIYers (and a growing legion of followers who covet it for it's health-giving properties in the bath and kitchen) seaweed is an invaluable way to return nutrients to the soil each year. There are however some "do's" and "don'ts" when it comes to seaweed foraging. The main thing is that you should never pull seaweed off the rocks. Remember that seaweed is a plant, and just like any other plant, if you pull away its root, it will die. Instead use a scissors and cut the plant, leaving about 6-8 inches behind, so that it will grow back. If we follow these simple guidelines, there will be plenty of seaweed to go around.

OVERWINTER CHILLIS

Chillipepper plants are not annuals at all and can in fact be overwintered and used again next year. This method is reputed to give you a better and earlier crop the following year. Dig up the plants carefully and remove any remaining fruit and foliage - cut the stem back to about 15cm. Pot up in some fresh potting compost and leave it on a sunny windowsill indoors - it won't survive outside. The plant will burst back to life in the spring and will produce fruit earlier than spring-sown plants.

COVER THE COMPOST HEAP

With wetter weather in store for the winter it makes sense to cover down your open compost heaps with layers of cardboard or carpet to keep in heat and keep out rain. It's a good idea to have two heaps - fill one and then leave it alone to rot down, then start filling the other and so on. You can add kitchen scraps but I would restrict this to veg peelings (there can be a surprising amount of these) and under no circumstances add meat or dairy as it will attract vermin.

Left: *Hen on slug patrol in the polytunnel.*

Right: *Nerdy soil fertility experiment using green and farmyard manure.*

Carrot and buttermilk soup with roasted carrots and dill oil

ROSS LEWIS

SERVES 8

FOR THE SOUP

250g onions, sliced

15g garlic cloves, finely sliced

125g butter

100ml rapeseed oil

200ml white wine

875g carrots, thinly sliced

150g beurre noisette

750ml water

1 litre chicken stock

3 star anise

¼ tsp coriander seeds

2 black cardamoms

¼ tsp black cumin

¼ tsp ground cinnamon

30g sugar

a little yuzu salt

FOR THE CARROT CRISPS

2 medium carrots, peeled

vegetable oil for deep-frying

From *Chapter One: A Story of Irish Food* by Ross Lewis. Published by Gill & Macmillan, 2013.

Soup

Sweat the onions and garlic in the butter and rapeseed oil in a large pan over a medium heat until very soft but not coloured. Add the wine and reduce by half, then add the carrots and continue to cook. Add the buerre noisette along with the water, stock, spices and sugar. Return to the boil and simmer for 20 minutes until the carrots are tender. Drain the carrot mixture through a colander into a clean pan. Reduce the liquid by half, then purée the carrots in a blender, adding back to the reduced liquid to make the soup. Season with the yuzu salt and a pinch of salt and then pass through a fine chinois.

Carrot crisps

Preheat a deep fat fryer to 140°C. Using a mandolin, finely slice the carrots, then deep-fry until crisp. Drain on kitchen paper and season with salt.

Chargrilled carrots

Place the carrots in a pan with the butter and dill. Add enough water to cover and simmer for about 40 minutes, until the liquid has almost evaporated and the carrots are cooked through and nicely glazed, tossing occasionally at the end to prevent them from catching. Preheat a griddle pan and brush with olive oil, then add the carrots and chargrill on all sides. Cool, season and cut into 5mm slices.

FOR THE CHARGRILLED CARROTS

100g baby carrots, scrubbed clean

50g butter

1 fresh dill sprig

a little olive oil

TO SERVE

240ml Cuinneog buttermilk

100ml cream softly whipped

10ml dill oil in a small squeezy bottle

Serving

Preheat the oven to 160°C. Reheat the chargrilled carrots in a roasting tin for 3-4 minutes until just warmed through. Heat 1.2 litres of the soup in a pan and when hot stir in the buttermilk. Blend the soup with a hand blender, adding the softly whipped cream. Divide the chargrilled carrots among warmed serving bowls and pour 180ml of the soup over each one. Finish with a tablespoon full of the cream, the carrot crisps and dots of dill oil.

Butternut Squash Fritters with Crumbled Blue Cheese

MICHELLE DARMODY

SERVES 2-4

a dash of olive oil

250g of butternut squash, peeled, deseeded and chopped into chunks

1 egg, lightly beaten

300 mls of milk

200g of self raising flour

1 tsp of baking powder

a small bunch of sage, finely chopped

100g of cream cheese

50g of blue cheese, crumbled

a handful of walnuts, toasted

a handful of pumpkin seeds

From Michelle Darmody of *The Cake Café* and author of *The Cake Café Cookbook*. Published 2012.

Toss the squash in a little oil and seasoning and roast in the oven at 180 degrees until tender. It will take about 20 minutes. Mash it once it has cooled a little. Whisk the egg and milk together until slightly foaming. Mix the flour and baking powder with a pinch of salt. Stir in the chopped sage. Make a well in the flour and stir the egg mixture into it, then stir in the cooled, mashed squash and the cream cheese.

Heat another dash of oil in a frying pan and put an eighth of the batter into it. Fry until golden underneath and then flip the fritter over. Continue with the rest of the batter.

Serve with the crumbled blue cheese, pumpkin seeds and the walnuts. A green leaf salad also works well on the side.

Chanterelle Mushroom Soup

CATHAL ARMSTRONG

SERVES 6

1 tbsp of butter

1 lb of chanterelle mushrooms

6 shallots, roughly chopped

2 garlic cloves

1 tsp fresh thyme, chopped

1 fresh bay leaf

½ cup chicken stock

1 quart cream

salt, pepper, nutmeg and cayenne

From Cathal Armstrong of *Restaurant Eve*, Alexandria, Virginia, USA.

Note: 1 quart = 950ml

Sweat shallots and garlic in butter until translucent. Add chanterelles and continue to sweat until all the liquid has evaporated.

Add chicken stock, cream, bay leaf and thyme and season to taste.

Continue to cook over medium heat for about 30 minutes.

Remove bay leaf, blend and strain through a fine mesh sieve.

Gnocchi with Jerusalem Artichoke and Pickled Mushrooms

DERRY CLARKE

Gnocchi features quite often on vegetarian menus, but you need to choose carefully what you serve with the gnocchi, as it can be slightly bland. This recipe uses pickled mushrooms, packed full of strong flavours. Jerusalem artichoke is a delicious but underrated vegetable that should be used more often.

SERVES 8 AS A STARTER

FOR THE ARTICHOKES

1kg (35oz) Jerusalem artichokes

2 litres milk

2 sprigs thyme

2 cloves garlic

FOR THE GNOCCHI

400g (14oz) flour

400g (14oz) warm baked-potato flesh, mashed

4 small or 3 large eggs

100g (3½oz) Parmesan cheese, grated

4 tablespoons parsley, chopped

salt and freshly ground black pepper

FOR THE MUSHROOMS

100g (3½oz) girolle mushrooms

100g (3½oz) trompette mushrooms

100g (3½oz) ceps

100g (3½ oz) portobello mushrooms

5 tablespoons olive oil

1 tablespoon chardonnay vinegar

2 tablespoons fresh tarragon, chopped

To prepare the artichokes, peel them and put them in a saucepan with the milk, the thyme and the garlic. Season with salt and freshly ground black pepper and simmer until tender, about 25-30 minutes. Remove from the milk and keep warm until you are ready to serve.

To make the gnocchi, sift the flour into a large bowl. Add the warm mashed potato, then the eggs, the grated Parmesan and the chopped parsley. Season with salt and freshly ground black pepper and form into a soft dough.

Divide the mixture into quarters and roll each quarter into a cylindrical shape. Divide each cylinder into six pieces. Lightly press a fork into the top of each piece.

Cook the gnocchi in batches in salted boiling water for 5 minutes. They are cooked when they rise to the top. They are now ready to serve, or you could brown them on a pan in a little oil for a different texture. Keep them in a warm oven until you are ready to use them.

To cook the mushrooms, clean and trim them and sauté them in a pan with the olive oil, chardonnay vinegar and chopped tarragon. Keep warm.

To assemble, divide the gnocchi, the artichokes and the mushrooms between eight starter plates and serve.

From *Keeping it Simple* by Derry Clarke. Published by Gill and MacMillan, 2009.

Baked Apples with Dark Chocolate and Cardamom

DORCAS BARRY

SERVES 4

4 large baking apples

seeds from inside of 8 cardamom pods

8 fresh dates, stoned and chopped

2 tbsp Highbank Orchard syrup (or maple syrup or honey)

juice from ½ a lemon

60g dark chocolate, chopped into large chunks

From Dorcas Barry at www.dorcasbarry.com

Preheat the oven to 180°C.

Wash the apples and core them. Using a sharp knife, score a line around the middle of each apple to stop the skin from cracking in the oven when they expand during cooking. Place into an ovenproof dish.

Grind the seeds from the cardamom pods in a grinder or pestle and mortar and mix in a bowl with the dates, syrup, lemon juice and dark chocolate. Spoon this mixture into the centre of the apples, pushing down with the thin end of a wooden spoon to fit as much of the filling as possible into each apple.

Bake in the oven for approximately 25-30 minutes, watching closely to make sure any overflowing chocolate doesn't burn.

Serve with natural yoghurt drizzled with some additional syrup.

Carrot cake

MAKES 1 CAKE

140ml vegetable oil, plus extra for greasing

3 eggs

220g light brown sugar

350g grated carrots

100g golden raisins

100g walnuts, chopped

200g self-raising flour

pinch of salt

$\frac{1}{2}$ teaspoon bicarbonate of soda

1 teaspoon ground cinnamon

1 teaspoon freshly grated nutmeg

FOR THE ICING

300g cream cheese, chilled

70g butter at room temperature

1 teaspoon vanilla extract

300g icing sugar, sifted

finely grated zest of 1 orange

FOR DECORATION

walnuts

orange zest

From *Clodagh's Kitchen Diaries* by Clodagh McKenna. Published by Kyle Books 2012.

Preheat the oven to 180°C/gas mark 4. Oil and line a 13×23cm loaf tin with greaseproof paper.

Beat the eggs in a large bowl, then add the oil, brown sugar, grated carrot, raisins and chopped walnuts. Sift in the rest of the dry ingredients and bring the mixture together using a wooden or large metal spoon until well combined.

Pour the mixture into the prepared loaf tin, smooth the surface and bake in the oven for 1¼ hours or until a skewer inserted into the middle comes out clean.

Remove from the oven and allow the cake to cool in the tin for about 5 minutes before transferring it to a wire rack to cool completely.

To make the icing, beat together the cream cheese and butter in a bowl until well combined. Add the vanilla extract, icing sugar and orange zest and mix until the icing is smooth and thick.

Use a palette knife to spread the icing evenly over the cooled cake, dipping the knife into a bowl of hot water if the icing is hard to spread out. Decorate the top of the cake with walnuts and orange zest.

December

MOST GIYERS ARE BUSY IN THEIR veggie patches right up to the end of November and of course come January we will be back to planning for spring. December however is another of the rare hiatus months in which we can take stock of this year's GIY achievements. There are jobs on the monthly to-do list but give yourself a break - much nicer I think to be perusing seed catalogues by the fire at night and dreaming of next year's growing.

I also like the idea of December as a month for celebration. Our ancestors have celebrated the passing of the shortest day of the year for over five millennia. In ancient Rome the winter holiday was called Saturnalia which honoured Saturn, the God of Agriculture. The pagans of northern Europe celebrated Yule (from whence we get yule-tide) in honour of the pagan Sun God Mithras. So we have ancient licence to celebrate the turn of the year with gluttonous feasting of epic proportions, so enjoy it!

The shortest day of the year is on the 21st of this month so if you're a 'glass-half-full' kind of person you can take solace from the fact that from then on the days are starting to get longer. Just as the harvest brings with it both joy and a measure of pathos at the impending winter, the arrival of winter brings, strangely, a sense of hope that it will soon be spring.

THIS MONTH'S TOP JOBS

* Add well-rotted manure or compost to beds and cover.

* Go on a course or read a book!

* Store leaves in bags to make leaf mould.

* Start planning next year's GIYing.

Things to Do in... *December*

PREPARATION

Continue digging over cleared vegetable beds and adding well-rotted compost or manure. Get educated – book yourself on a course over the winter! Start a veg patch diary – a fantastic learning tool and makes for great reading later on! Start planning what you would like to grow next year including at least one previously untried vegetable. Order seed catalogues and study them before deciding on the best varieties to grow to suit your needs. Start a compost corner or heap. If you don't already have one, plan a fruit garden/area to include at the very least some soft fruit like raspberries, strawberries, gooseberries and currants; and some fruit trees like apple, plumb and pear.

TO DO LIST

Good garden hygiene helps greatly in the prevention of disease carry-over from one year to the next so remove yellowing leaves from any crops remaining and rake up fallen leaves. Mice can be a problem at this time of the year and crops sown in the ground over winter like broad beans, garlic etc. can be vulnerable. Protect them under cloches. It's a good time of the year to add lime to your beds (particularly the ones that will take brassicas next year), so buy a pH testing kit if you don't already have one, and test your soil. Keep an eye on your stored veggies and discard anything that's rotting – I generally empty out the boxes of sand that I have carrots and beetroot etc. at least twice over

Above: *Holy Sh*t!*

winter to check them out. Do interesting things with leaves! Store in bags to make leaf mould or use as cover for bare soil (keeps weeds down and prevents drying out).

SOWING SEEDS AND PLANTING OUT

If you haven't already done so plant garlic – traditionally in the soil by the shortest day of the year, but I typically wait until early spring to sow mine. Bring herbs like mint, chives, lemon balm, parsley and thyme indoors by lifting and potting them up.

HARVESTING – WHAT'S IN SEASON?

In general terms it's back to winter vegetables (and stores, if you have them) but you can try bucking the seasonal trend by continuing to harvest winter salad leaves (if you were canny enough to plant them in August or September) like corn salad, land cress and mizuna. You should still have at least some produce left in the December veg patch for example: winter cabbages, Brussels sprouts (of course), leeks, kale, chard, perpetual spinach, Jerusalem artichokes, celeriac and parsnips. By now I have generally lifted for storage: carrots, celeriac, pumpkins, squashes, potatoes, onions, beetroot and garlic. Happy Christmas!

Veg of the Month - Garlic

WHY GROW IT?

Most of the garlic available in supermarkets here is imported from China (over 5,000 miles away!), which is particularly odd considering it's relatively easy to grow and stores extremely well. It's also incredibly good for you. The garlic requirements of an average family can be easily satisfied by even the smallest of vegetable patches. If you were to take any bulb of garlic, break out the cloves and stick them in to the ground spaced about 10cm apart, each clove would eventually turn in to a bulb of garlic. That's the magic of it. However it is recommended not to use supermarket garlic for this purpose as it can bring disease in to your soil (if you are going to do this, sow the garlic in containers). Buy certified disease-free garlic from a garden centre or online.

SOWING

Most GIYers sow garlic in early winter (Oct-Dec, but before the shortest day of the year – Dec 21st) as the bulbs benefit from a cold snap. Some varieties however can be sown in early spring, and that's generally when I sow mine. Pick a sunny site, with good fertile, free-draining soil. Apply an organic fertiliser (like chicken manure pellets) before sowing. Sow each clove just below the surface, spaced about 20cm apart, in rows 25cm apart. If soil is very wet, sow in module trays and transplant when sprouted.

GROWING

As with onions, garlic hates weed competition so keep the bed weed free. Hoe carefully around the bulbs every week or so. Water occasionally in dry weather but don't over-water.

Left: Did you hear the one about the Chinese garlic? If not, you can read all about it on page 10!

HARVESTING

Harvest once at least half to two-thirds of leaves on each plant are yellow-brown. Autumn sown garlic will be ready in early summer. Spring sown garlic won't be ready until August. Do not allow them to go too far as they lose flavour. Lift carefully and dry on racks in sun (or indoors in wet weather) for two weeks. Hang in plaits.

GIY RECOMMENDED VARIETIES

Early Wight, Solent Wight, Vallelado, Printanor (spring planting).

PROBLEMS

Rust can affect leaves but it shouldn't affect bulbs. White rot (as per onions) is more serious as it attacks the root. No remedy – do not grow garlic in that soil again for 7 years.

GIY TIPS

- Sow garlic before shortest day of year and harvest before the longest day.
- Remove any flowers that form on stems while growing.

MONTHLY INSIGHT – TOOLS FOR GIYING

I've learned a couple of fundamental lessons about food growing over the years – one of the most important is that it's important to (a) have the right tools and (b) spend money to acquire good quality ones. Cheap tools are a complete waste of time and money.

GIY'S TOP 5 TOOLS

Hoes – hoes changed my life! You will have read throughout this book that hoeing is the best way to stay on top of weeds in the veg patch, ultimately saving you time and effort. I hoe almost every week in the veg patch whether it's needed or not, prevention being better than cure. I have three hoes – an oscillating hoe for larger weeding jobs and a small headed Dutch hoe for getting in around onions etc. The ridging hoe is for earthing-up potatoes so it's a slightly different animal, but very effective. I also have a hand-held hoe for even more precise jobs and for digging out stubborn weeds.

Spade – a good sharp, stainless steel spade will cost upwards of €50 but it's worth paying the money for a decent one, which will last for a decade or more. I give mine a good clean with the hose each time I use it, and always store it in the potting shed. The sharp blade makes light work of digging and composting.

Fork – there are lots of different forks you can buy – I have a good quality 4-pronged fork that I use for turning over soil, turning the compost heap and spreading compost on beds.

Rake – raking is important in the veg patch particularly for the beds where you are sowing seeds direct (e.g. carrots and parsnips) and you need a fine tilth. In my veg patch I have a mix of raised beds and standard 'open' veg beds - in the open beds I use the rake to tidy up the beds and paths.

Hand tools – I have numerous little tools on hand in the potting shed – a stainless steel hand trowel is important for planting seedlings; a hand-fork is good for breaking up the soil surface to reduce compaction; a dibber is a handy tool for creating small holes for seedling planting; tape measure – the nerd in me likes neat and well-ordered beds and accurate spacing!

CARING FOR YOUR TOOLS

- Don't leave them outside to get rusty – I store all my tools standing upright in the potting shed.
- If you think of it, wash tools after use particularly if weather is mucky and they are coated in soil.
- Sharpening the blades on your spade and hoe in the winter months will keep the tools in peak condition.
- Rubbing some linseed oil in to the handles once a year will prevent them from getting brittle and breaking.

DECEMBER TIPS

BUILDING A RAISED BED

Firstly, decide on your bed design and where you are going to put it. A 1.2m (4ft) square bed is ideal as you will be able to reach in to the centre of it from all sides (therefore never having to stand on the soil which would compact it). 25-30cm deep is traditional. Measure out the lengths of wood needed, cut them to the size and nail together. Bear in mind that when filled with soil there will be quite a bit of pressure on the sides of the bed so nail the planks to pegs (driven in to the soil with a mallet) for support. Place a good thick layer of wet cardboard and newspaper on the surface of the grass - it will kill the grass and weeds off and then break down to improve the soil. Fill the bed with alternating layers of manure/compost and top soil - aim for a mix of 60% soil and 40% compost/manure.

HOW LONG DO SEEDS LAST?

There's nothing more frustrating than poor germination of seeds - particularly if you don't know WHY the seeds didn't germinate. Sometimes, it can be due to the fact that the seeds are past their use-by date. Parsnips are a classic example of a seed where you really should be buying new seed every year because the seeds are perishable. Here's a rough guide to how long you can keep different veg seeds:

1 year approx: parsnips, beetroot, leeks, sweetcorn, peppers (sweet and chilli), spinach, onions, parsley.

2-4 years: squash and pumpkin, courgette and marrow, beans and peas, carrots.

4 years +: Brussels sprouts, cabbage, cucumber, kale, lettuces, radish, tomato, turnips.

DIVIDE AND CONQUER

You can divide rhubarb plants every four or five years to give the plants more room and reinvigorate them. The best time to do this work is now while the plant is dormant. Dig the rhubarb using a fork to lever the crown carefully from the soil. Remove any rotting sections from the plant and give it a general clean up. Then using a sharp spade, press down heavily and divide the crown in three. Ideally you want each section to have a crown, a large amount of root and at least 4 or 5 pink buds. Then dig a hole for each divided crown and place the crowns, roots downwards, with the top of the crown roughly an inch BELOW the soil surface. You can pop some well-rotted manure or compost in to the hole first if you want to add some nutrients. Backfill with soil, firming in gently.

BRUSSELS SPROUTS

Pick sprouts as soon as they are ready to eat (while still hard and firm and before they open out). Pick the sprouts from the bottom of the stem first and then move upwards. To harvest a sprout simply snap off by pulling downwards. The leaves at the top of the stems can be cooked like spring greens – very tasty they are too. Do not "Irish mammy" the sprouts by boiling the divil out of them for 20 minutes. Blanch them in boiling water for just one minute and then fry them in some oil with a sliced clove of garlic and some almond flakes. Season well and add some olive oil before serving.

Roast Garlic Colcannon

Colcannon is a traditional Irish dish made from mashed potato and cabbage or kale. By roasting the garlic in this way, its flesh is tempered and tamed to become sweet and mellow.

SERVES 4-6

1 large head of garlic, left whole and unpeeled

2 tbsp olive oil

salt and ground black pepper

1 sprig of rosemary

1kg (2lb 3oz) floury potatoes, unpeeled

450g (1lb) Savoy cabbage or kale

250ml (9fl oz) milk

50g (2oz) butter

From *Entertaining at Home* by Rachel Allen. Collins 2010.

Preheat the oven to 220°C (425°F), Gas mark 7.

Place the whole head of garlic in a small ovenproof dish, drizzle with olive oil, season with salt and pepper and add the sprig of rosemary. Cover with foil and cook in the oven for about 45 minutes or until the garlic has completely softened.

Place the potatoes in a large saucepan and cover with cold water. Add a good pinch of salt, cover with a lid and bring to the boil. After 10 minutes strain off two-thirds of the water, put the lid back on the pan and cook over a gentle heat so that the potatoes steam for about 30 minutes until they are tender.

Remove and discard the dark tough outer leaves from the cabbage (if using). Wash the rest and cut into quarters, removing the core. Cut the cabbage or the kale across the grain into slices about 7mm thick. Place in another large saucepan, add the milk and simmer for about 4 minutes or until tender.

When the potatoes are just cooked, peel and mash them while still warm with the butter and some salt and pepper. Use your fingers to squeeze out the roasted garlic pulp and beat into the potatoes with enough boiling milk from the cabbage to make a fluffy purée. Then drain the cooked cabbage or kale, stir into the mash and taste for seasoning.

For perfection, serve immediately in a hot dish with a lump of butter melting on top.

Beetroot and Carrot Gratin

MICHELLE DARMODY

SERVES 4

300g of waxy potatoes,
sliced very thinly

4 carrots, sliced

3 beetroot, peeled and sliced

a small bunch of rosemary,
pulled from the stalk and
chopped

4 cloves of garlic, sliced

250ml of cream

70g of Parmesan, grated

mixed salad leaves for four

a handful of almonds,
toasted and chopped

1 tbsp of vinaigrette
dressing

From Michelle Darmody of *The Cake Café*
and author of *The Cake Café Cookbook*.

Lay the sliced potato, carrots and beetroot into an ovenproof dish,
sprinkling the garlic and rosemary between layers.

Pour the cream over the whole lot and place into an oven heated to 180
degrees until the vegetables are soft which will take about 40 minutes.
Season and sprinkle with the parmesan and place back into the oven
until golden on the top.

Toss the leaves and almonds in the dressing and season. Slice the gratin
in four and gently transfer onto a plate. Serve with the salad on the side
and with some chutney if you wish.

Cauliflower with Cheese Sauce

CATHAL ARMSTRONG

SERVES 4-6

1 medium cauliflower
(approx 1lb)

2 oz butter

2 oz all purpose/plain flour

large pinch salt

1 pint milk

1 cup cheddar cheese or
similar, grated plus extra for
sprinkling on top

freshly ground pepper

From Cathal Armstrong of *Restaurant Eve*,
Alexandria, Virginia, USA.

Heat the oven to 195°C/385°F.

Remove the green outer leaves from the cauliflower and steam whole over a pan of boiling water for 10 minutes. Remove the cauliflower from the heat and leave to cool.

Place the butter and flour into a large saucepan. Over a low heat stir the butter and flour until the butter has melted and the flour is incorporated. Add the salt and mustard powder and continue stirring for 2 minutes.

Turn the heat up to medium and add the milk in one go and whisk furiously until a smooth sauce is formed. Continue stirring until the sauce is thickened and glossy (about 5 minutes). If the sauce is very thick add a little more milk. The sauce should be thick, but still runny. Add the grated cheese and stir until melted. Remove from the heat.

Break the cauliflower florets from the thick, central stalk, taking care not to break it into tiny pieces.

Place the florets in a baking dish large enough to hold all the florets in one layer.

Pour the thickened cheese sauce over the cauliflower, ensuring all the florets are covered. Sprinkle with grated cheese and a good twist of black pepper.

Bake in the hot oven until the sauce is bubbling and golden brown on the top, approximately 30 minutes.

Butternut Squash and Coriander Seed Bread

This is an unusual but unbelievably delicious and moist bread – the squash gives it a fabulous colour and the seeds add to the texture. This moist bread has the most beautiful colour and should be enjoyed fresh on the day it's made. Otherwise, freeze it when it's fresh and it will keep for up to 3 months.

MAKES 1 LARGE LOAF

1 small butternut squash (about 700g), cut into wedges

sunflower oil

salt and freshly ground black pepper

1 lemon, zest only

2 tbsp honey

1 tsp coriander seeds, lightly crushed, plus extra to decorate

2 ½ tsp dried yeast (or 1 x 7g sachet)

1 tsp sugar

280ml lukewarm water, more if required

650g '00' or strong white flour

½ tsp salt

1 egg, beaten

From *Catherine's Family Kitchen* by Catherine Fulvio. Published by Gill & Macmillan Ltd 2011.

Preheat the oven to 180°C/fan 160°C/gas 4.

Place the butternut squash wedges in a lightly oiled roasting pan and drizzle with oil. Sprinkle with salt and pepper and roast for about 35 minutes, until golden and softened. Remove from the oven and set aside to cool. Once cooled, scoop the flesh from the skin and place in a bowl. Add the lemon zest, honey and coriander seeds and mash until smooth.

Mix the yeast and sugar in the lukewarm water and allow to activate. When the yeast is frothy, it's ready to use.

Meanwhile, sieve the flour and salt into a bowl. Add the yeast mixture as well as the butternut squash mixture, making sure you have enough liquid to form a soft dough. Knead on a floured surface for about 10 minutes, until smooth. Cover and leave in a warm place for about 2 hours, until it has doubled in size. The time will depend on the time of year and the temperature of the room.

Divide the dough into 2 pieces. Using the base of your hands, roll into two 30cm-long ropes.

Grease a baking tray with sunflower oil. Twist the ropes together, pinching them together at the ends. Cover and leave in a warm place until doubled in size, which should take about 1 hour.

Preheat the oven to 200°C/fan 180°C/gas 6.

Brush the loaf with the beaten egg and sprinkle with the coriander seeds. Bake for 25-30 minutes, until the bread sounds hollow when tapped on the bottom. Allow to cool on a cooling rack.

Apple Galette

This tart is so pretty and versatile. You can use any type of fruit or berries. Blueberries, plums, apples, blackberries and rhubarb all work really well. If pastry isn't your thing then this tart is a great place to start as the pastry is almost dough like and very forgiving; Part of its charm is its rustic look!

SERVES 8

THE PASTRY:

200g plain flour

140g cold butter, cubed

25g sugar

1 egg

THE FILLING:

70g (2 ½oz) almonds

1 tbsp plain flour

70g (2½oz) butter

60g (2oz) caster sugar

1 egg

3 eating apples

1 tbsp milk

1 tbsp brown sugar

From *Make Bake Love* by Lilly Higgins, published by Gill and MacMillan, 2011.

Preheat the oven to 190°C.

Put the flour in a bowl. Rub in the butter until it resembles breadcrumbs. Stir in the sugar, mix in the egg.

Knead quickly and shape into a disc, cover with cling film and place in the fridge for 10 minutes.

Next make the filling. Put the almonds and flour into a food processor and blitz. Add the butter and sugar. Blitz again. Add the egg and blitz till it's a smooth paste.

On a lightly floured surface roll the pastry to form a 30cm circle. Place onto a large greased baking sheet.

Spread the almond mixture over the pastry. Leave a border around the edges.

Thinly slice the apples. Layer them in a nice pattern and then fold up the sides of the pastry to keep the almond mix and apples safely inside.

Brush the edges with milk and sprinkle with sugar. Bake for 25-30 minutes until golden.

Leabharlanna Poiblí Chathair Baile Átha Cliath
Dublin City Public Libraries

INDEX

ACKNOWLEDGEMENTS

There's always a risk when you put down on paper all the people you want to thank on a project like this - that you end up leaving people out and offending them. With the sincere hope that I don't do that, here goes.

First of all, a huge thanks again to all our contributing chefs, cooks and growers who so generously provided their recipes and their enthusiasm for this project. Also, a huge thanks to their publishers for allowing us to re-produce the content in this book, and to the photographers for use of their wonderful photographs.

Self-publishing a book is not easy, since it involves taking on much of the work that a publisher normally does. It's even more challenging on a book like this, where there were nearly 40 individuals contributing. My hare-brained idea of having so many contributing chefs and using only seasonal veg-focused recipes, left Cristíona Kiely with a monumentally complex editing job – like putting together an enormous jigsaw (with me coming in and out every now and then to re-arrange the pieces!). Throughout the process I was pushed, questioned, charmed, pushed again, challenged, cajoled, flattered and pushed some more – whatever the situation demanded! I can never thank her enough for her tireless commitment to the project and her grace under fire.

To our wonderful designer Lucy Parissi, thank you for your incredible patience and wonderful design work. Fair to say you just "got" this project right from the start, which made it much easier. Thanks Jessica Reid for sub-editing work and Mícheál Ó Cadhla for the loan of your eagle eyes for proofing. The final bank holiday weekend of proofing will live long in the memory!

On a project like this it's vital to have a wise and thoughtful advisor at the end of the phone – Fran Power has been a great friend to us over the years on various GIY publications, and gave us great advice again this time around. Thanks Fran! Other conversations also proved very important, notably with Lizzie Gore-Grimes, Klaus Laitenberger and Simon Pratt at Avoca, giving me the confidence to push on at rather anxious moments.

Thanks Paul Sweetman and Ciaran Walsh for all your advice on the "pounds, shillings and pence", and to my board at GIY for your support. Thanks also to our friends and supporters in the GIY movement for being a constant source of inspiration and support. A massive thanks also to the amazing team that work in GIY and GROW HQ – evidence if ever it was needed how mountains can be moved by a small group of people with passion and shared purpose.

Finally, but most importantly, to my own family – Eilish, Nicky and Vika – for your patience, but above all your love.

PHOTO CREDITS

A huge contribution to this book was made by numerous photographers and food stylists (amateur and professional) and we are hugely grateful to them for their work and allowing us to use their images. In particular we would like to credit the following:

Patrick Browne - *Michael Kelly*, page 80.

Joleen Cronin - *Sally and John McKenna*, page 185.

Mark Diacono - *Celeriac and Lemon Thyme Crème Brulée*, page 44, *Cauliflower Pakoras with Raita*, page 97.

Kevin Dunne - *Rachel Allen*, pages 38 and 166.

Eat Good Food Group - *Cathal Armstrong*, page 272.

Nancy Forde - *Denis Cotter*, page 63.

Rich Gilligan - *Michael Kelly*, page 11.

Kieran Harnett - *Derval O'Rourke*, page 122.

Trevor Hart - *Raw Kale Salad*, pages 42 and 43, *Bean and Kale Soup*, page 76, *Dorcas Barry*, page 77, *Baked Apples with Dark Chocolate and Cardamom*, page 255.

Lilly Higgins - *Spiced Beetroot and Potato Rosti*, page 226.

Leona Humphreys - *food styling in Rhubarb recipes*, page 101.

Jason Ingram - *Mark Diacono*, pages 45 and 96.

Aaron Jay - *Alys Fowler*, page 123.

Jorg Koster - *Denis Cotter*, page 205.

Dan Moloney - *Imen McDonnell*, pages 143 and 229.

Jane Powers – *Joy Larkcom*, pages 162 and 232.

Donnie Phair - *Neven Maguire*, pages 182 and 202.

Koster Photography - *Darina Allen*, page 230.

Photos by Jen - *Biddy White Lennon*, page 138.

Barry McCall - *Domini Kemp*, pages 61 and 139, *Derry Clarke*, pages 98 and 254, *Marian Keyes*, page 145 and 215, *Ross Lewis*, pages 168 and 248, *Rachel Allen*, page 269.

Imen McDonnell - *Blackcurrant, Lemon-Vanilla Verbena glazed tart*, page 142, *Wild Chanterelle, Caramelised Onion, Caraway and Buffalo Cheese Galette*, page 228.

Sally McKenna - *Channeled Wrack and Ginger Miso Slaw*, page 184, *Gubeen and Wild Sea Beet Pizza with Seagrass*, page 120.

Joanne Murphy - *Lilly Higgins*, pages 140, 227 and 276.

Diarmuid O'Donovan - *Nessa Robins*, page 213.

Seamus O'Neill - *Michael Kelly*, page 246.

Shane O'Neill - *Rhubarb recipes*, pages 101.

Grace O'Sullivan - *seaweed*, page 131.

Nessa Robins - *Blackberry and Apple Cobbler*, page 212.

Deirdre Rooney - *Trish Deseine*, pages 58 and 188.

Alistair Richardson - *Marian Keyes' Mam's Apple Tart*, page 214, *Sweet and Simple Strawberry Cupcakes*, page 144.

Donal Skehan - *Nettle Soup with Wild Garlic Oil*, page 117, *Deep Fried Courgette Flowers*, page 157, *Sharon Hearne Smith*, page 190, *Teeny White Chocolate Pistachio and Raspberry Tarts*, page 191.

Mike Smallcombe - *Hugh Fearnley Whittingstall*, pages 134 and 158.

Scott Suchman - *Cathal Armstrong*, page 252.

Dylan Vaughan - *Eunice Power*, pages 100 and 102.

Simon Wheeler - *DIY Pot Noodle*, page 135, *Chard and New Potato Curry*, page 159, *Alys Fowler*, pages 141 and 209.

Kate Whitaker - *Spiced Butternut Squash and Coconut Soup*, page 40, *Clodagh McKenna*, pages 41 and 256.

Notes

Notes

  Notes

Notes

  Notes